WRITERS AND THEIR WORK

ISOBEL ARMSTRONG
General Editor

ANITA DESAI

ANITA DESAI

Elaine Yee Lin Ho

NORTHCOTE
BRITISH
COUNCIL

© Copyright 2005 by Elaine Yee Lin Ho

First published in 2005 by Northcote House Publishers Ltd, Horndon, Tavistock, Devon, PL19 9NQ, United Kingdom.
Tel: +44 (0) 1822 810066 Fax: +44 (0) 1822 810034.

British Library Cataloguing-in-Publication Data
A catalogue record for this book is available from the British Library

ISBN 0-7463-1051-X hardcover
ISBN 0-7463-0983-X paperback

Typeset by PDQ Typesetting, Newcastle-under-Lyme

Printed and bound by CPI Group (UK) Ltd, Croydon, CR0 4YY

Contents

Biographical Outline

1937   Born on June 24 in Mussoorie, a hill station north of Delhi, to a German mother, Toni (formerly Nime), and a Bengali businessman, D. M. Mazumdar.

1957   Awarded BA in English literature after studying at Miranda House, Delhi University.

1958   Marries Ashvin Desai, a businessman. Has four children, Rahul, Tani, Arjun and Kiran, who is also a novelist.

1963   Debut novel, *Cry, the Peacock*, published in Britain by Peter Owen, publisher of literature from the Commonwealth and continental Europe.

1964   *Voices in the City* published by Peter Owen.

1971   *Bye-Bye, Blackbird* published by Peter Owen.

1975   *Where Shall We Go This Summer?* published in Delhi by Vision.

1977   *Fire on the Mountain* published in Britain by William Heinemann.

1978   *Fire on the Mountain* wins the Royal Society of Literature's Winifred Holtby Memorial Prize and the National Academy of Letters Award, Delhi. *Games at Twilight and Other Stories* published in Britain by William Heinemann. Desai wins Sahitya Akademi Award in India.

1979   *The Peacock Garden*, a children's book, published in Britain by William Heinemann. *Games at Twilight* published by Harper & Row, US. *Where Shall We Go This Summer?* awarded the Federation of Indian Publishers and Authors Guild of India Award for Excellence in Writing.

1980   *Clear Light of Day* published in Britain by William Heinemann. Novel is shortlisted for the Booker Prize.

1982   *The Village by the Sea*, a children's book, published in Britain by Puffin.

1983   *The Village by the Sea* wins the Guardian Children's Fiction Award.

1984   *In Custody* published in Britain by William Heinemann, and Harper & Row, US. Novel is shortlisted for the Booker Prize.

1988   *Baumgartner's Bombay* published in Britain by William Heinemann. First novel to be written outside of India while Desai is resident at Girton College, Cambridge.

1993   Appointed John E. Burchard Professor of Writing with the Massachusetts Institute of Technology's Program in Writing and Humanistic Studies. Awarded the Neil Gunn Prize for International Literature from the Scottish Arts Council. Film of *In Custody* released, directed by Ismail Merchant, screenplay by Desai.

1995   *Journey to Ithaca* published in Britain by William Heinemann.

1999   *Fasting, Feasting* published in Britain by Chatto & Windus, and Houghton Mifflin in the US. Shortlisted for the Booker Prize.

2000   *Diamond Dust and Other Stories* published in Britain by Chatto & Windus, and Houghton Mifflin, NY. Awarded the Alberto Moravia Prize for Literature.

2002   Retires from MIT.

2003   Appointed Sidney Harman Writer-in-Residence at Baruch College, City University of New York. Receives Padma Shri Award from the Indian Government.

Abbreviations and References

BY ANITA DESAI

BB   *Baumgartner's Bombay* (1988; London: Vintage, 1998)
CLD   *Clear Light of Day* (1980; London: Vintage, 2001)
FF   *Fasting, Feasting* (1999; London: Chatto & Windus, 1999)
FM   *Fire on the Mountain* (1977; London: Vintage, 1999)
GT   *Games at Twilight and Other Stories* (1978; London: Vintage, 1998)
IC   *In Custody* (1984; London: Vintage, 1999)
JI   *Journey to Ithaca* (1995; London: Vintage, 2001)

BY RABINDRANATH TAGORE

HW *The Home and the World* (1915), trans. Surendranath Tagore (1919), repr. with Introduction by Anita Desai (London: Penguin, 1985)

Introduction

Of German Indian parentage, Anita Mazumdar Desai was born and grew up in India. Since the 1950s, she has lived in New Delhi, Calcutta, Bombay and other Indian cities, until the early 1990s when she began to spend part of her year in the United States. She started publishing her work in India soon after her marriage to Ashrin Desai in 1958. In a writing career which has spanned more than four decades, Anita Desai has agreed to few interviews, and in them she has shown a marked reticence about her own personal life. In an interview in 1988, shortly after the publication of *Baumgartner's Bombay*, she was asked about her mixed parentage, and while affirming her self-identification as 'totally Indian' and that India has been her 'whole world', she also drew a rare connection between her maternal – and German – upbringing and herself as Indian: 'I am able to look at a country I know so intimately with a certain detachment, and that certainly comes from my mother because I'm aware of how she would have reacted to people and to situations. I feel about India as an Indian, but I suppose I think about it as an outsider.'[1]

The notion of thinking as an outsider, and the detachment or critical distance which this entails, is a key to an understanding of Desai as writer, and will be a recurrent theme in the discussions of her novels and short stories in this book. It informs her authorial perspectives on India, its places, scenes, and people, and her creative engagement, through narrative, with those who, through a combination of accident and choice, find themselves marginalized, displaced, and dispossessed. In the interview, Desai traces her fascination with the outsider to notable instances in her early reading: 'I remember the first time I read Camus' *The Stranger*, what a tremendous impression it

1

made on me. There was a time when I read that book over and over again. ... Dostoevski was the other writer I think who interested me so much when I was young. And again it was this other-worldliness of his characters.'[2] The search for other, alternative, worlds outside the social and cultural mainstream defines the self-identity of many of Desai's characters, and underlines their problematic identification with the communities in which they are located.

If Desai writes about an India that might be occluded to those who live, or profess to live, within the Indian mainstream, it is also one which is often inaccessible to readers outside India. For a foreign reader like myself, who has only visited India once, and whose experience of 'India' is mostly mediated by Indian friends who live abroad, reading and writing about Desai's work pose fascinating challenges. In a brief interview in 1984, the year when *In Custody* was published, Desai observes, 'a book is made not only by the writer, but by its readers as well. The writer has his conception, but the reader gives it different interpretations ... and so the book leads a life beyond the one given it by the writer. Reading a book is like travelling in a new country, and the reader-traveller may be well or poorly equipped.'[3] In the light of Desai's comments, a further possible connection can be made between her characters as outsiders and the reader as outsider. Desai's fictions take the reader, on visit after visit, to ordinary places and into unremarkable households that are transformed, in the course of narrative, into haunts of strangeness inhabited by characters who exist vertiginously between routine and the anxiety – and often tragedy – of estrangement. From the vantage of her own 'homeliness' in India, Desai's fictional 'India' is the space of the unhomely (*unheimlich*). In the bond of their repeated contact and engagement with the unhomely, author and reader become fellow travellers on a journey through those quotidian and yet imagined spaces which constitute 'India'.

Through gardens and streets, homes and ashrams, and from cities to remote villages, the sea to the mountains, Desai locates each site through realistic details of flora and fauna, making them known as natural environments while weaving into her descriptions symbolic perspectives on her human subjects and their perplexed lives. There is a carefully observed animal and vegetable life in her fictional places, but Desai's natural interests are almost always anthropocentric: 'No life stirred at this arid time of day – the birds still drooped, like dead fruit...some squirrels lay limp on the wet earth under the garden tap. The outdoor dog lay stretched as if dead on the veranda mat, his paws and ears and tail all reaching out like dying travellers in search of water' ('Games at Twilight', *GT* 2). They speak of and speak to the geography of feelings and familial relations unfolding in the narrative. The dog figured at the beginning of the short story, 'Games at Twilight' finds its human counterpart in a sort of narrative rhyme near the end, in the character of the boy Ravi, who, coming out of his place of hiding, discovers that the game of hide-and-seek which he thinks he has won is long over. In the twilight, the other children move like a funereal group, 'the heads bowed so sadly, and their feet tramped to that melancholy refrain so mournfully, so helplessly that Ravi could not bear it...He lay down full length on the damp grass, crushing his face into it, no longer crying, silenced by a terrible sense of his insignificance' (*GT*, 10–11). The story, told over ten pages, is not as melodramatic as the parallel drawn above would suggest, though it is useful to remember that in many of Desai's works, passion and its violence burst the seams of gentility to enforce a dubious closure upon a straitened sense of self and strained human relations. In 'Games at Twilight', the common features of the garden and children at play are deformed so that both reappear in the half-light between the living and the dead.

While the mapping of natural and ethnographic features locates a specific narrative in place, Desai is much less forthcoming about when it takes place – that is to say, its particular historical conjuncture. Each of the eleven stories collected in *Games at Twilight* (1978) marks the time of its own occurrence, but they are also ahistorical in that they cannot readily be referred to a chronology, and even less to specific events, of contemporary India. We see this again in the novella, *The Village by the Sea* (1982), published after *Games at Twilight* and subtitled 'An Indian Family Story'. Though the short stories have an urban setting, and the novella is set in rural India, both narrate lives in domestic time, far removed from the sort of references to political time which underpin, for instance, Rushdie's novels. This is true of most of Desai's fiction before

Baumgartner's Bombay where the titular character is Jewish, an ethnic outsider, and where 'India' is situated in world historical time from the Second World War to the present. But it is equally arguable that through the narrative of Baumgartner's arrival and life in Bombay, Desai incorporates world historical time as 'Indian' time, and domesticates it. We know most of Desai's works are set in post-independence India but the transitions between colonialism and independence, which Rushdie so consciously plays on, are embedded in the histories of the characters or glanced at obliquely as the turbulent backdrop in which these histories are placed. 'India' in Desai's fiction is the hours, days, and years of 'India' at home, even though that homeliness is haunted by spectres from the past, and disrupted by the tumult of the everyday present.

India in the world, the world in India – Desai is emphatic that her characters speak not only of their specific historical and geographical locations, but to the suffering and tragedies of the human condition. Referring to *In Custody*, she observes, 'this book does contain my view of humanity and society and the world, and what I have observed of it. That it is also my view of India, of Indian society and Indian life, is merely a coincidence ...'[4] And in response to another question about the unrelieved misery of Baumgartner's existence, she says, 'I see his condition as not being one of extraordinary suffering, but of suffering which fits in with the general scheme of things. The subject of all my books has been what Ortega y Gasset called "the terrors of facing, single-handed, the ferocious assaults of existence." ... Hugo is not a representative of the Jewish race to me but of the human race, of displaced and dispossessed people and tribes all over the world.'[5] While Desai's vantage on the tragedies of estrangement and unbelonging looks back to her mixed ancestry and informed reading of literary predecessors, her fiction plots an outstanding contour in the late twentieth century – and postcolonial – map of diasporic, exile, and migrant imaginations. The 'assaults of existence' are universal, but 'displaced and dispossessed people and tribes' have been displaced and dispossessed by particular historical circumstances. Individual and domestic tragedies and comedies may be shaped by global forces, and may in return give to these forces a human name and meaning.

1

At Home in India

With the publication of *Fire on the Mountain* (1977), *Games at Twilight* (1978), and *The Village by the Sea* (1982), Desai became more widely known to western readers, first in Britain and then in continental Europe and the United States, and began to confirm her reputation outside India. These three works map out the spaces of an 'Indian' milieu which include the rural precincts of Kamala Markandaya and the domestic interiors of Attia Hosain, and compare well with the acute observations of small-town Indian life for which R. K. Narayan's Malgudi novels are renowned. Desai's passage from India also brings her 'India' to the world; alternating between urban and rural settings, the three works offer tantalizing glimpses of the rich variety of lives, locales and cultures in post-independence India, and enter into the inner sanctums of families, communities, and individual psyches.

But as much as they reveal, there is also a distinct reticence which is partly attributable to the brevity of the works themselves – *Fire on the Mountain* and *The Village by the Sea* are novellas, and *Games at Twilight* is a short story collection. As a formal quality, this reticence suggests Desai's careful reappraisal of her craft after the tortuous lengthiness of the earlier novels.[1] This is particularly evident in *Games at Twilight* which figures as a quasi-laboratory of narrative experiments focusing on character, situation, or event, and where different points of view of narration are tried out and manipulated. The reticence also speaks to an understanding – and a respect – for the mystery of human existence and circumstance which the author explores and probes through her imagination but can never fully comprehend, represent, or narrate. It is characteristic not only of these three earlier works but also of the full-length novels that Desai was to publish later on in the 1980s, and which secured

5

her fame. Its recurrent function is to unsettle any complacent assumption of knowledge about 'India' garnered from a reading and rereading of her works, and to put the reader in her place, so to speak, between familiar recognition and encounter with an impenetrable unknown. It is tempting, though not necessary, to name this reticence as 'Indian' for it is a quality which Desai shares with the greatest of modern short story writers like Joyce and Katharine Mansfield, and earlier, Chekhov. Historically, the short story form, as a European literary genre, developed as a counter-discourse of little narratives against the epical grand narratives which dominate the nineteenth century. In being graphic and expressive, and in being brief, the three works look, in one direction, towards Desai's own location in India as creative inspiration, and in another, towards her inheritance of the English short story as a world literary genre.

Games at Twilight can be subtitled 'Sketches of India'. The stories, eleven in all, take the readers into domestic interiors behind the closed doors of Indian households, revealing ordinary families in meagre circumstances or middle-class comfort, and offer poignant insights into marriages and family relations in varying degrees of sickness and health. The titular story, 'Games at Twilight', and 'Pineapple Cake' explore a child's contact with adult anxieties – distressing for the child, who can only intuit that such contact represents a life-affecting transition. These stories play on the gap between the child's intensely felt but barely understood experiences and the reader's knowing perception of the loss of innocence they signify. Two stories, 'A Devoted Son' and 'Surface Textures', are about characters whose views and actions are closely observed by the other characters, members of their family and immediate community, but whose motivations and interiority remain undisclosed. The reader is kept in the dark, reading what the other characters read, sharing their mystification, and with recourse only in speculation about the essential mystery of individuality itself. 'Studies in the Park' and 'The Farewell Party' represent the claustrophobia of middle-class Indian life in its conformity to norms of social success – academic achievements, professional and community status – and the rituals that safeguard and calibrate the performance of these norms. In these two stories, as in 'Pigeons at Daybreak' with its recurrent images of suffocation, Desai turns a very critical eye on the notion of community itself as it is realized in the everyday pressures upon individuals who have to, or feel they have to, live up to the demands of those closest to them, and the consequent frustrations they suffer about loss or dispersal of self in myriad others. The struggles against privations of self are grounded economically in 'Private Tuition by Mr Bose' and 'Sale', two stories in which the commodification of their literary or artistic talent is keenly felt by the protagonists themselves who, fighting against the slide into poverty, can find little relief in familial affection or sympathy. 'The Accompanist' narrates the relationship between master and pupil, a theme which Desai will elaborate in *In Custody*, arguably her most accomplished novel about Indian life, which will be discussed in detail in chapter 3 of this book. 'Scholar and Gypsy', the last story of the collection, has as its main characters two Americans who are visitors to India, and again, I will return to the issue of the foreigner in India, and how it is situated in relation to Indian characters, later on, in chapter 4.

The main characters in the ten stories never live alone; they are surrounded by family, and beyond that the village or the press of people in their familiar habitat. But home is seldom haven or refuge, and community is more often than not the bonds of obligation from which the passage of time brings no reprieve. Caught in a net of relations, the characters are nonetheless always isolated, living lives of resignation, *ennui*, and restless discontent which reach breaking points in the making of the stories' narrative crises. As one reads the stories, gradually a common pattern begins to take shape. In each, there is the building up of an intolerable situation till it reaches a moment of breakdown that is often also cathartic release. What follows is a transformation, ranging from shifts in perception to a sea-change where the character becomes unrecognizable to those around them. These transformations are often poetically rendered, in a language of abstraction which intervenes in the dominant realistic discourse, and speaks implicitly of alternative realms to which individuals, in moments of crisis, are afforded access or – for the very few – totally translated. If 'India' is often seen (more popularly so at the time when *Games at Twilight* was published than now) as the domain of the spiritual and the mystical and religious strife, then what Desai has shown in these stories is how the spirit, as abstraction or transcendence from the real, enters through a process of change so that lives that are plain or on the edges of despair are invested with a new meaning. It is important to realize, however, that such change, sometimes gradual, often abrupt, is detached from the rituals associated with particular religious or cultist practice, and not justified in institutionalized religious doctrine or philosophical belief. In this respect, the short stories show an 'India' where the humblest individuals can be transformed in spirit, and yet which is, in many ways, remarkably religion-free.

The pattern of narrative, deceptively simple, and in many ways conventional, is belied by the skilful manipulation of narrative point of view. To coordinate a discussion of point of view – or Desai's craft – with the thematic issue of transformation, I would like to look at three stories from *Games at Twilight*: 'Studies in the Park', 'Surface Textures' and 'The Farewell Party'. 'Studies in the Park', narrated in the first person, begins with a section of free indirect speech which pries open the interiority of the main character, Suno. In this opening section, Suno, a young student, describes the incessant clamour which surrounds him at home as his father listens to the news in Hindi, Tamil, Punjabi, and Gujarati, his mother 'cuts and fries, cuts and fries', chops and slices, and a succession of neighbours, in voices that 'clash, clatter and break' (*GT* 20) descend upon the house. The description is, of course, not objective, for it embeds Suno's frustrated reaction, bordering on hysteria, to the family milieu in which he seems unable to find a moment of peace and quiet, and where the injunction, 'Suno, Suno, study for your exam' (*GT* 20) sounds a shrill recurrent note in the dense texture of cacophonous sounds. Right from the start, Desai assembles and foregrounds a lexicon of sounds as the signifiers of Suno's first-person perception of his environment, his internal state, and the story's thematic and figurative meaning. To augment this, the relations between Suno and his family are figured, in the young student's fevered imagination, as cannibalistic activity – he imagines his mother slicing and feeding him to his brothers and sisters.

The rest of the story narrates Suno's escape from home, and moves from the domestic space to the tea-shop, the street, and then the park. The differences between home-space and the other spaces are textualized by the change in quality and level of noise. In the tea-shop, the proprietor whines, the waiter murmurs and babbles; on the street, the *gram* vendor speaks 'in a friendly voice. Not insinuating, but low, pleasant' (*GT* 23), and noticeable calm returns to Suno's observations of and response to his surroundings which continue to be detailed and charged with creative energy. Entering the park, Suno also moves imaginatively from the quasi-barbarism of home to a sub-magical space where old men look like 'wizards and bogey-men', old women are 'bag-like', and a 'madman or two' prance round like monkeys. Noise is displaced; instead there is varied activity, among which other students, like Suno, studying for exams, stroll up and down, reading, murmuring to themselves, until they come to rest in the shade of trees. It is in the park, 'quiet, almost empty' in the afternoons, that Suno is replaced in some sort of community, and a kind of equanimity of spirit descends.

In configuring shifts in Suno's point of view with the contrasts between sounds and silence, Desai unfolds character, social relations, and the varied spaces of a specific local and urban geography. The reprieve which Suno experiences in the park is, however, temporary; it is but a short lull in the slow passage towards a kind of death. Or at least it seems so to Suno who, in thinking of himself as dying as the examination draws ever closer, has reached the furthest limit of where the burden of an imposed identity as student can be endured: 'I didn't work myself any more – I mean physically, my body no longer functioned. I was constipated. I was dying' (*GT* 29). This is part of the narrative build-up towards the ultimate transformation, or transfiguration, that is to take place. In the penultimate moments, Suno witnesses a scene in the park which will bring about a radical disjunction between his present and future identities, and the decisive break with the past: 'Then I saw the scene that stopped it all, stopped me just before I died' (*GT* 30).

In the scene, there are two main figures: a young Muslim woman, in a black *borkha*, lifts her veil with a 'pale, thin hand' to reveal a face 'like a flower, wax-white and composed' as she lies in the lap of a very old man with 'spectacles and a long grey beard like a goat's or a scholar's' (*GT* 30). Beside them are two girls playing. What strikes Suno about the woman is her whiteness and her beauty, and between young and old, woman and man in this quasi-familial scene, he discerns a tenderness of feeling that he has never before felt at home, and is nothing short of revelatory. The tableau of the still and composed figures and contrast of primary colours is iconic, and Suno's mesmerization is akin to that of an initiate into a mystery of existence and state of being. This experience he can only compare to gazing 'at a painting or a sculpture, some work of art' (*GT* 30), a comparison which suggests how Desai, with authorial reticence, draws back from identifying the experience as religious vision. The fact that the woman is a Muslim is a sideways glance towards religion that is displaced, or at least disoriented, by Suno's re-presentation of the experience as artistic. What is foregrounded, through the comparison, is a pointed authorial indication of an active – or overactive – imagination being liberated from its entrapment in everyday reality to a different order of aesthetic illumination.

Here is a crisis which can be read as breakdown, transformation, or enlightenment; Suno does not probe the psychology of his own experience, and an understanding of its nature remains closed to the reader. What is shown is that the change in him that follows when he refuses to take his exams and thus totally rejects his identity as student is not explained or explicable in the terms of the quotidian reality of which his baffled parents are the guardians. All we see is the change itself, and Suno's acceptance that 'life has taken a different path ... in the form of a search' (*GT* 32). The first-person narrative reveals but also limits what is revealed, to forestall a closure which brings full disclosure; the story ends with a new beginning, in the ambivalence of a search without teleology as Suno wonders if he will get 'another glimpse of that strange vision that set me free. I never have but I keep hoping, wishing' (*GT* 33). A single revelatory experience that is life-transforming but that is not repeated: there is an interesting cross-reference to be drawn here between Suno's story and what Desai says in an interview where she is asked about the source of inspiration of her work, whether it resides in her understanding of people. She replies: 'It's not always understanding. Sometimes simply trying to understand, hoping for that moment of revelation, but often it's simply a search or a quest with no goal in view.'[2] In Suno's first-person narrative of transfiguration, 'Studies in the Park' can be read as an early attempt by Desai to embody and place in everyday life an insider's understanding of that rare and singular moment of revelation that is the zenith of an artistic quest.

'Surface Textures' represents another attempt to understand a process of radical and dramatic change but this time from the outside; in the story, the third-person narrator describes and observes the main character, Harish, on whom the change is wrought, and this external perspective is further dispersed through alternating character focalizations. In the beginning, the third-person point of view is frequently mapped onto that of Harish's wife, Sheila, whose discontent becomes the measure of his perceived inadequacies and incomprehensible departures from domestic norms. Their relationship is faltering because they seem to inhabit two different orders of material reality – the 'surface textures' of the title. While Sheila shops and frets about prices in the markets, and cooks and serves at home, Harish is 'captivated' by physical objects which he singles out, for no apparent reason, from their familiar domestic surroundings. At the dining table, he strokes a 'big button of a yellow melon' which seems 'puny' to Sheila and 'boring' to their children, running 'his fingers up and down the green streaks that divided it into even quarters as by green silk threads, so tenderly'(GT 35). He says little; in fact, his only utterance in the entire story is restricted to two exclamations of 'Oh, no' near the beginning. What is shown is that he is a keen observer of objects, his eyes roving and hunting all around him until they rest

> not on things on which people's eyes normally rest...but on such things, normally considered nondescript and unimportant, as the paving stones on which their feet momentarily pressed, the length of wire in a railing at the side of the road, a pattern of grime on the windowpane of a disused printing press. (GT 36)

Unable, it seems, to concentrate on his allocated tasks, Harish is dismissed from his government job. At first hysterical, Sheila soon leaves with the children to return to her paternal home, and disappears from the story. Harish is evicted from his flat, and for a while his neighbours lose sight of him, till he is spotted as a vagrant on the railway platform 'staring across the criss-cross of shining rails' (GT 38). The last section of the narrative reports his behaviour and actions – how he walks as if he is

11

'feeling the earth carefully', and seems to investigate and worship the very rocks he sits on, each 'having a surface of such exquisite roughness, of such perfection in shape and design, as to keep him occupied and ecstatic for weeks together'. It is in the rocky and barren land outside the town that he finds his 'especial paradise' (*GT* 39). Confronted with such alterity, the townspeople, his former community, undergoes a change in perception. Mothers, not unlike his wife Sheila, proclaim him a Swami, put before him offerings of food and milk, and beg him to speak. Harish remains silent, and in his silence is even more revered and worshipped.

Harish is keenly observed, both by the third-person narrator and by other characters, none of whom seems any wiser than the others about his inner states. They can only watch and describe his appearance and actions and form their own judgements, first of his ineptitude and then, in a complete reversal, of his sanctity. In other words, Harish, obsessed with surfaces and textures, is also, as character, composed entirely of surfaces. His interiority is a closed book, or the remarkable gap at the centre of the narrative.[3] This is a real feat of technical daring at the other extreme from the expressive first-person narrative in 'Studies in the Park'. It is also superbly coordinated with a narrative of non-conformity which embeds philosophical questions about relations between surface and depth, and the paradox that surface – as everyday life, observable behaviour, and what is available to the senses – is the only plane on which the profoundest truths may be made manifest, represented, and accounted for. And as in 'Studies in the Park', where a transformed Suno finds eventual accommodation within a different space in his community, Harish's alterity, in being named Swami, is acknowledged and replaced among his own people. 'India', in these two stories, is not only a place where the spirit enters to transform individuals and to unsettle and dislocate the small communities to which they belong, and cause communal strife, but also a place where such strife can be and is resolved as part of everyday life.

In these two stories, and others in the collection, Desai shows the tensions within the family which are linked to the presence of the family *in* community, a fact of social existence in which the perceived need to live up to communal standards of normality and success generate intolerable pressures upon parent–child and husband–wife relations. Within these strained relations, women, as wives and mothers, figure as both harasser and the harassed. Suno's mother and Harish's wife, in their very conventionality, appear as adverse and uncomprehending others to their son's and husband's difference, but it is also the case that they are themselves driven to distraction. While some kind of equilibrium returns to the community when all passion is spent, it is always the family, dysfunctional to begin with, which suffers irreparable loss. In 'The Farewell Party', Desai further explores the problematic of the family in community from another different perspective: that of the woman, as mother and wife, who is estranged from those social duties expected of someone of her class and station in life.

The main character, Bina, is married to Raman, a company man in an Indian town who is about to leave for a new posting in Delhi. The story, narrated in the third person and free indirect style, is about the scene of the garden party which Bina hosts for other women and their husbands, the only and last occasion of its kind during the five years her family lived in the town. It focuses on Bina's awkwardness and discomfort in playing hostess, and flashes back to scenes which show her general aversion to joining the charity work and recreational past-times of the other company wives for which she 'had a kind of sad contempt and certainly no time' (GT 83) since the burden of child-caring, especially of a severely spastic son, has entirely devolved upon her in the family. Not quite a social pariah but certainly a woman who does not belong, and cares little about belonging, outside the circle of family and the hospital where she takes her son, Bina, at the party is recurrently astonished by her guests' exclamations of affection which suggest relations of closeness, even intimacy, and a recognition of her family's standing in the small community. The narrative follows her thoughts as she circulates among the guests, and her shifting memories of their brief encounters; in this dutiful ritual of farewell, she is constantly reminded of earlier rituals of sociation she has not performed that belie the others' effusive expressions of regret at her imminent departure. At the same time, the community which seems belatedly to embrace her as family is, from her estranged optic, distastefully

13

familiar. There are recurrent indications, through external description and narrative focalization through Bina's point of view, that a critical intelligence is at work in piercing the façades of bourgeois respectability.

Bina is described as 'a frigid and friendless woman' but also as having 'a certain presence, a certain dignity' (GT 83); this is how the external world, mediated by the third-person narrator, sees her, and is a measure of her refusal to wear those masks required for social belonging. At the party, forced to prepare a face to meet the faces that she meets, the narrative constitutes Bina as subject in that gap between the inner self and the cultural mask that ill-fits her.[4] When she confronts the masks of familiarity donned by her guests, Bina averts her gaze which reveals too much about her inner self beneath her own inadequately prepared face. In response to the lament of Mrs Ray, the Commissioner's wife and the town's social doyenne, at their leaving after only two years, Bina, 'widening her eyes', utters a single word – 'Five' – and is herself 'surprised at such a length of time' (GT 84); then she 'gazed down at her hands'. When Mr Bose from the local museum declares his admiration for her success as mother, she 'was flustered by this unaccustomed vision of herself and half-turned her face away' (GT 86).

Bina's position is an uncomfortable one, and in following Bina through the party, Desai also unfolds the psychological duress that this position entails. While 'Surface Textures' points towards the strains that financial hardship puts on the wife and marriage, 'A Farewell Party' explores the fissures in middle-class society made invisible by material well-being and rituals and activities of sociation which allocate wives their places. In the gap between Bina's brief, awkward responses to the guests and her inner thoughts, the narrative shows the self-repression that she is forced to practise in order to 'fit in', if only on this one occasion. To stay within the family domain is the only alternative world available to her, and although 'her back [was] almost literally broken' (GT 84) by the duties of child-care, it remains the channel for genuine self-expression. At a moment near the end of the story, just before the guests depart, Bina glimpses her daughter in 'the lighted drawing room ... the cynosure of all juvenile eyes, having thrown herself with abandon into a dance of monkey-like movements' (GT 93).

Her daughter's 'abandon' is in obvious contrast to Bina's inhibition but it is also the discreet measure the text offers of her achievement as mother in providing an environment at home that enables her child to inhabit the company of peers in a way she herself cannot. Having shown Bina as socially disabled for most of the narrative, the point of view is subtly reversed to provide a flash of insight into what she has enabled.

This prepares for the ending in which, after most of the guests leave, Bina and Raman join the few remaining, the doctors from the hospital and their wives 'who had held themselves back in the darkest corners and made themselves inconspicuous throughout the party' (GT 96). If the dark recesses of Bina's inner self are what she has kept hidden from prying external eyes, it is also in the unnoticed and symbolic darkness of the garden that her true community waits. Care replaces commerce; Bina is relocated among a class of professionals in a space alternative to the company men and their wives that constitute the mainstream middle-class community dominating most of the narrative. The fusion of the self and community, and its belated visibility is emblematized by one of 'Tagore's sweetest, saddest songs' sung by one of the wives.[5] The ritual of song replaces the ritual of the garden party, and this alternative community is drawn together at the very moment of departure and dispersal. As with a number of the other stories, 'The Farewell Party' ends ambivalently, resonating of both beginning and ending.

In her social and psychological dislocation, Bina represents a version of the woman subject recurrent in Desai's work, and through the making and remaking of this woman subject, Desai explores 'India' at home as it revolves around the challenges women face in their traditional and allocated positions, and their struggles to liberate and transform their lives. These experiences may not carry the mystical overtones that we see in 'Studies in the Park' and 'Surface Textures' but they are no less historically significant in that they map the routes of continuity and change in everyday life, that order of reality in which most of Desai's characters, and certainly her women, live their fictional existence. Before turning to a more detailed exploration of Desai's women subjects in the next chapter, I would like to discuss briefly *The Village by the Sea* because this novella raises at least two interesting questions about how Desai conceptualizes and locates 'India' at home.

The stories in *Games at Twilight* all have urban or suburban settings in which middle-class subjects, in relative degrees of poverty and wealth, predominate. *The Village by the Sea* is an attempt at representing rural life in a poor fishing village, but its subtitle, 'An Indian Family Story', clearly suggests that it is no less about life in India, as it is lived in the private spaces of the family, than the stories in *Games at Twilight*. Indeed, the subtitle goes further to suggest that the rural family is, in some ways, typical or representative; though presented as fiction, Desai is at pains to explain the real-life referentiality of her narrative. In a statement facing the opening page of the novella, she says, 'This story is based entirely on fact. Thul is a real village on the western coast of India and all the characters in this book are based on people who live in this village; only their names have been altered.' Although some of Desai's other fictions depict rural scenes and locations, *The Village by the Sea* significantly represents the only attempt in her *oeuvre* to date to focus exclusively on rural life, and it is in this context that the statement about Thul's factuality appears most intriguing. No such statement prefaces the middle-class fictions of *Games at Twilight* or the other novels until *Fasting, Feasting*. In addition, *The Village by the Sea* is dedicated to three members of the Mayadas family 'whose house in Thul provided [Desai] with many holidays and all the material' for the book.

Desai might have felt a need to address the issue of how as an outsider, and a tourist or holiday-maker, she can write about or speak for the villagers in Thul. In venturing out of the bourgeois home-ground, familiar to herself and her readers of Indo-English fiction, Desai faces the challenge of writing about an India that she can only have indirect knowledge of, and in an artistic genre and a language remote from, if not entirely unknown to, its inhabitants.[6] This is a challenge that Indo-English creative writers who are Desai's contemporaries, and those before and after her, recurrently confront.[7] In his author's foreword to *Kanthapura* (1938), a novel set in an Indian village, Raja Rao, writing a generation before Desai, discusses the issue of representing rural life at the heart of Indian culture in an alien language. Fluently bilingual, Rao maintains that writers like him 'cannot write like the English' and 'cannot write only as Indians', but their 'method of expression ... has to be a dialect' which reflects a doubled-optic on their home in the world. This well-rehearsed argument has been taken up by writers from other postcolonial locations,[8] but it really side-steps the problematic question of representation which he and Desai, especially as realist writers, could well have encountered. The final paragraph in Rao's essay is worth quoting in full because it presents a kind of closure on his argument that actually deflects the question. After commenting on how the episodic nature of his narrative imitates traditional Indian story-telling, he concludes:

> It may have been told of an evening, when as the dusk falls, and through the sudden quiet, lights leap up in house after house, and stretching her bedding on the veranda, a grandmother might have told you, newcomer, the sad tale of her village.[9]

The images, lyrically charged, compose an everyday moment of Indian life in a rhetoric designed to evoke and demonstrate the possibilities of referentiality through English. This symbolic rhetoric is further justified through the image of the story-teller, the grandmother figure who is the emblem of tradition. In ascribing the authority of narrating to her, Rao subtly shifts his role from author-creator to that of the scribe who records an orature presumably in an indigenous language by one whose first-hand experience of the culture encoded in that language is above question. While the responsibility for creating the story is displaced from Rao himself, the story itself is authenticated. If the grandmother-narrator is agent and witness of indigenous culture, Rao, in retelling the story, is alibi. At the same time, Rao shores up his role as cultural translator in naming the addressee of the narration: the 'newcomer'-reader, not necessarily foreign but definitely an outsider to both oral and rural traditions mediated by the indigenous language. In a further and final gesture of self-authentification, Rao can be seen to be inviting the reader to think of him as the grandmother-narrator. What we are offered in the essay is a fascinating glimpse of an exemplary transaction between an Indo-English writer and his place in Indian life and literature which hinges on a rhetorical negotiation and orchestration of his multiple identities as author-creator, transcriber, and translator.

Some of this complicated transaction is played out in the novel's subtitle and Desai's statement that Thul is a real place, and that the characters in *The Village by the Sea* are based on real people. In making the statement, her story, presented as fiction, is authenticated in history, and located in place. Her outsider perspective on the lives of the Thul villagers is implicitly acknowledged but the hesitation about the authority of this perspective is circumvented for, like Rao, she assumes the role of quasi-ethnographer and cultural translator who makes known to the English-language world an indigenous Indian community which has so far remained invisible to its view. The subtitle further glosses the rural Thul story as typical, and links it, in its 'Indian-ness', with the narratives of bourgeois Indian families in *Games at Twilight*. But despite these manoeuvres, there is a suggestion that Desai continues to be discomfited by her only narrative of rural India. When questioned in an interview about the happy ending of *The Village by the Sea* six years after it was published, she admits that while the story 'is based on a real family... their lives didn't end as happily' as in the book. She accepts the interviewer's description of the novella as 'a fairy tale', and explains, 'I wrote it that way for children. I felt immensely dissatisfied with it and admitted to myself that I would have written it quite differently if I hadn't been writing it for children.'[10] Poised on the sharp edge between the quest for authentification – or referentiality – of her rural tale, and creative self-determination to mould genre and real-life material, her predicament remains unresolved.

There is an alternative perspective on this comparison between Rao and Desai which will take us into another area of inquiry about Desai's representations of 'India'. Rao's concluding images of the village at dusk and the grandmother-narrator suggest how the bond of community, enacted in the daily ritual of story-telling, lies at the heart of Indian society and culture itself. In making this point, Rao can be seen to be to reaffirming in detail Tagore's idealized comments on Indian life:

> Because her homes, her fields, her temples of worship, her schools, where her teachers and students lived together in the atmosphere of simplicity and devotion and learning, her village self-government with its simple laws and peaceful administration – all these truly belonged to her.[11]

As E. P. Thompson observes, Tagore 'had a clear conception of civil society, as something distinct from and of stronger and more personal texture than political or economic structures. In [Tagore's] view... civil society in India had survived as an organic reality.'[12] We have already caught a glimpse of Desai's reference to Tagore in the song at the end of 'The Farewell Party', precisely at the moment of community formation, and there are recurrent references to Tagore's writings in other Desai novels and essays. In their characters, representations, and narrative, Desai's fiction, including *Village by the Sea*, enact in fiction some of the relations and practices that enable and guarantee Tagore's vision of civil society. What emerges from her fiction is, of course, a far less idealized picture, for Desai also underlines the forces that undermine, disrupt and threaten the existence of civil society. This is as much the function of her critical distance from a society and world that is very different from the time of Tagore's 1917 lecture, as of a different discourse and rhetoric.

But in remembering Tagore in her own writing, and in her detailed narrative of Indian life and the lives of foreigners in India – which will be further discussed in the following chapters – we can see not only civil society and its discontents but also an enduring interest in the legacy of Tagore's commitment, evident in the 1917 lecture, to a liberal humanist universalism which attempts to transcend the division between east and west, what is national and what is alien. That this interest often translates in Desai's work into an optic on tragedy and ruin or irony and ambivalence about the idealistic – as in the 'fairy-tale' – also suggests her acute realist comprehension of those domestic and communalist rivalries that had shaped Tagore's commitment in the first place, and that endure not only in India, but also in the world's recognition and imagination of 'India'. The other dynamic of this commitment, that of inter-cultural and international rivalries, mobilizes not only the narrative of the foreigner in India, but also Desai's imaginative passage, in her later works, outside the territorial boundaries of India as nation-state, and into the world. Tagore is remembered in Desai's works but while memory conjures a poetically rendered idealism, or the hopes of the past, it speaks as frequently and with tragic poignancy to failure and futility in the present.

2

Women in India

In an article entitled 'A Secret Connivance', Desai criticizes 'a subtle, deep-rooted form of suppression' in India and she attributes this connivance to the denial of education to women, and hence their complete dependence on men for their livelihoods and sense of themselves and their social place.[1] 'Like other countries where women are traditionally suppressed,' she observes, 'India deifies its women', as mother goddesses and loyal wives devoted to their husbands as lords and masters. An Indian girl is brought up on myths and legends celebrating these archetypes, and inculcated with the belief that her mission in life is to try and live up to them, even 'if in reality she is nothing but a common drudge, first in her father's house and then her husband's'. She cannot speak out or rebel because to do so is to question the myths and legends, 'the cornerstone on which the Indian family and therefore Indian society are built'. This is a situation for which men are not entirely to blame, for Desai sees women as conniving in it, and she attributes this connivance to the denial of education to women and, hence, their complete dependence on men for their livelihoods and sense of themselves and their social places. In classical poetry of the oral tradition by women poets, this predicament is encoded in the recurrent theme of a woman pining for a man, often camouflaged as 'the pining of the soul for the godhead, a spiritual longing'.[2] Through the article's exposé of the interpellation of the woman subject, and the hidden dynamics of gender relations, Desai shows how the material privation of women is justified in a complex of ideological expressions which constitute India's cultural inheritance. Indians themselves, according to Desai, 'have been as guilty' in creating and perpetuating these notions which shield both themselves and readers in the West from truths about 'the human being within', and a quotidian reality which is often seen as dull and unexciting. Desai concludes:

> If literature, if art has any purpose then it is to show one, bravely and uncompromisingly, the plain face of truth ... Once you have told the truth, you have broken free of society, of its prisons. You have entered the realm of freedom.[3]

Reading this article and Desai's fiction in the context of each other, it can be argued that her short stories and novels perform acts of truth-telling about India; there is an implicit textual politics in her fictional work that aligns with the social criticism of the article.[4] In this performance, she enacts not only the courageous attempts of individuals to emancipate themselves from inherited cultural and social bonds but also her own freedom as artist; the shifting contours of everyday life throw up new locations of truth, and constitute the fertile ground of fiction itself. In her fictional revelations about the truth of women's lives in India, Desai shows that for her women characters, 'at home' in India all too frequently means the confinement to a domestic milieu, and the bearing of an intolerable cultural tradition. This is the experience of Nanda Kaul in *Fire on the Mountain*, published a year before *Games at Twilight*, and Bim and Tara in *Clear Light of Day*, Desai's first major – and critically acclaimed – novel. These women protagonists have connived in their own imprisonment in the sense that Desai has argued in the article, for they have accepted the grind of domesticity in a familial and cultural situation when other choices do not seem available or the opportunity for seeking them out does not arise, and being an outcast is unthinkable. The struggle to transform home from prison to some semblance of expressive private space is the measure of the women's agency and selfhood. In this struggle for liberation, memory is often the key, both as it turns the lock which can shut and open the prison gate. The novels locate these women in the present and, from this point in time, narrate their past – as memory triggered consciously or unconsciously, or by external reminders – in its haunting of their daily lives, forever unsettling 'home' with the 'unhomely'.

The desire for emancipation from the past as bondage, and the quest to see her life truthfully and see it whole underline the narrative of Nanda Kaul in *Fire on the Mountain*. In this novella, Desai explores the genealogy of the desire, its nature, and tragic outcome in the chaos of the inner self, the trauma of loss and betrayal, and ultimately, in death. The conduct of Nanda Kaul's quest for truth, half-willed and half generated by the force of circumstance, takes the form of interior monologues for most of the novel; as in the short stories, there is minimal dialogue, which is a characteristic Desai technique to suggest the breakdown of social relations. Nanda Kaul's withdrawal into the recesses of the self is symbolized by her lonely house, Carignano, high on a ridge above the town of Kasauli, which has a troubled history all through colonial and postcolonial times, in the same way as Nanda is haunted by her memories. The description of Carignano's past focuses on its women inhabitants and the violence visited upon them or which they inflict on others. In its recent history, a succession of British spinsters, the subject of strange passions, have lived there, their lives as isolated as the house and as semi-barren as the landscape itself or the garden which they try but fail to grow. Their relations with the native inhabitants down the hill in Kasauli are at best tempestuous, and at worst fatal, as symbolized by the death of a coolie whose head was sliced off by the iron roof blown off the house during a thunderstorm.

After 1947, the house was no longer considered safe for single women, and they retreated with the imperial tide, their 'virginity intact, honour saved, natives kept at bay' (*FM* 9); Kasauli 'went native' (*FM* 10), and Nanda bought the house. The novel clearly wishes to suggest that Nanda is the latest in the line of a dubious female inheritance at an outpost which is the reserve of the most marginalized of imperial women subjects. In this inheritance, the novel situates Nanda's struggle for self-transformation in the context of changes and continuities in woman's social situation from colonial to postcolonial times. The novel not only exemplifies Desai's interest in interiority but can be read as a psychoanalytic narrative which takes into account the impact of history and culture upon an individual's sense of identity. For Nanda, Carignano is meant to be a new beginning; this personal transition, like the momentous historical change from colonialism to independence, holds forth the promise of emancipation but has to contend with a past which turns out to betray in its deepest consequence.

Turning her back on her life as the wife of the vice-chancellor in a provincial university, and her two married daughters, Nanda came to Carignano to seek inner peace and self-renewal. In describing Carignano as 'the wild world of female space', Geeta Ramanathan argues that Nanda's desire for total isolation in the wilderness displaces a complex of former experiences she cannot articulate, and that her external composure belies a disordered, inchoate, or 'wild' sense of self that the third-person narrator recurrently draws attention to, and which the free indirect style pointing to Nanda's interiority augments.[5] One of Desai's characteristic strategies in the novel is to suggest symbolic correspondence between Nanda's inner state and the physical environment and ecology of the Kasauli hills. Nanda desires to be 'a charred tree trunk in the forest... She would imitate death, like a lizard' (*FM* 23). One can read this as a desire to return to nature, or to be transformed into part of the environment, to reintegrate the human self into the ecological system. However, in this desire, there is also paradoxically a death-wish, and it is through this death-wish that the text undermines the promise of Carignano as present and future. It traces this wish back to the past in showing how Nanda 'had practised this stillness, this composure, for years, for an hour every afternoon' (*FM* 23) when she locked herself in her own room, and yet could not escape the irritating noises of house-hold movements and activities. Though she appears to enjoy the privileged social status of vice-chancellor's wife and hostess, Nanda has to suffer the betrayal of her husband's long-term affair with Miss David, the mathematics teacher at the college, and her domestic life is a turmoil of frenzied activity, suppressed frustration, and interiorized chaos.

Although at Carignano, she seeks freedom from the past, she cannot help but conjure this chaos. In a backward reference to her old home where she is aroused from her daily, self-imposed isolation, or called back to life, so to speak, by family duties, the text shows a moment when the silence round her is broken first by the cry of the cuckoo with its 'domestic tone' (*FM* 19), and then the shrill voice of her friend, Illa Das, down the phone, speaking of a possible visit. Unable to escape from Illa's voice, she watches a white hen 'drag out a white worm inch by resisting inch from the ground till it snapped in two. She felt like the worm herself, she winced at its mutilation' (FM 21). The text recurrently shows Nanda as the observer of her immediate physical environment in order to suggest a persistent desire to locate a new self in its present place, but the images of observed nature carry ineluctably the burden of past memory and its fatal consequence upon the self. If the desire to be still and isolated embeds a death-wish, then the image of the mutilated worm suggests that to be forced back into the society of her past would be to continue in a life where the self is violated and broken. Nanda's sojourn at Carignano is precarious; the house is the no-man's land – or the woman's space – haunted by the death-wish and death-in-life.

In seeking isolation, Nanda is subject to the illusion that her earlier self, deranged by marital and domestic chaos, can be transformed, and become the building blocks of a new interior domain that is composed and fulfilled. One of the models of such transformation is inscribed in the ancient Japanese narrative *The Pillow Book of Sei Shonagon*, which she reads from time to time, and the text quotes a fragment from the book entitled 'When a Woman Lives Alone', which offers counsel about her habitat. It 'should be extremely dilapidated, the mud wall should be falling to pieces' (FM 27), the pond overgrown with water-plants, the garden sprouting weeds – this clearly appeals to Nanda, and represents the wilderness, both exterior and interior, she desires in Carignano. In the narrative of a woman's turn from society to nature, the Japanese classic reads like a kind of manual for living a single life in which physical space expresses a deliberately cultivated notion of making disorder the principle of a new order. Behind the façade of the 'natural', what the text proposes is a relationship between the woman and her environment that is highly mediated by art – or artifice – to the extent that it can be formulated and formalized. Paradoxically, the domain of disorder institutes its own conventions – or chaos has its own theory – but though Nanda desires the paradox and seeks its practice at Carignano, she does not have the art. She is a reader, not an author, and Carignano, as its history of desolation and violence shows, is a place which

defies human cultivation and composure. In this history is
inscribed the doom of her project of self-transformation and
self-creation.

At the same time, Nanda's incapacity as author-creator is
embedded in her history as a mother who has always found
child-caring a burden, and whose daughter and grand-
daughter are both disappointments to her. Her daughter, Asha,
she considers vain and obsessed with social status, and Asha's
daughter, Tara, is an abused wife who has had recurrent
nervous breakdowns. Asha's letter to her mother about Tara's
latest collapse reminds Nanda of those maternal responsibilities
that she has tried to perform, and the outcome in failure of that
life-long performance. In the imminent arrival of Raka, her
great-granddaughter, whom Asha has no time for and Tara
could not look after in her illness, Nanda sees her failure as
mother repeated in her progeny. To Nanda, Raka's physical
presence and proximity are unsettling. As observer-reader once
again, Nanda watches, at first with irritation and then envy,
Raka's ease in finding a foothold in Kasauli as though she
belongs naturally to the landscape and ecology of the desolate
hillsides. Her great-grandchild is like 'an insect' in its element;
in Raka's long absences from the house she sees her own wish
'to be left alone and pursue her own secret life amongst the
rocks and pines of Kasauli' (FM 48).

In another paradoxical twist characteristic of the novel, Raka
also appears as the self uninhibited by social constraints which
Nanda so much desires. This begins when Nanda first perceives
the sameness and difference between herself and Raka – they
are both recluses, but Raka, unlike herself, 'had not arrived at
this condition by a long route of rejection and sacrifice – she was
born to it, simply' (FM 48). In this perception, Nanda's irritation
at Raka gives way to admiration, and she is implicitly drawn
back, through her great-granddaughter, into some identification
with family and her own past. Speaking with Lalita Pandit about
their childhood experiences of Kasauli, Anita Desai says,

> Kasauli is a place where I spent summer once as a small child and
> experienced the place as Raka does, who went on her own, in
> solitude to explore the place. But that is an experience one can lose
> as an adult. When you write about the experience as an adult, it
> ceases to have that mystery as well as the immediacy. It took me

years and years to recover that. I did when I took my children there, and seeing them play on the hillside, wander around the pine woods, somehow brought back my own experience to me very vividly.[6]

A romantic notion of childhood seems to inform these observations – as it does Nanda's perception of Raka as the child in nature. Adulthood represents the loss of immediacy in an individual's experience of place, an immediacy which cannot be brought back but can be recollected in tranquillity or conjured when a sensation of that experience is made available once again through present observation. In the parlance of psychoanalytic criticism, Raka appears to Nanda as the Imaginary stage of infancy and early childhood antecedent to individual incorporation into the symbolic and patriarchal social order which, for Nanda, has been the 'long route of rejection and sacrifice'. Raka figures as the return of the Imaginary, a disruption to the symbolic order which Nanda herself is trying to break away from – a difference, a model, and an alternative. The problematic and duplicitous role of memory is fully revealed in the Nanda–Raka relationship: it is a prison-house into which Nanda is thrust back or forced to return when Raka breaks her isolation at Carignano; it is also the key to the pre-symbolic, that woman space of self-imagination and self-liberation.

The narrative of Nanda's observations of Raka is fragmented, and dispersed in episodic chapters throughout the novel. In this narrative, Raka is sometimes present, observed by Nanda, but frequently not; Raka appears and disappears unpredictably, out of the control of Nanda's consciousness and her incipient othering of her great-granddaughter. This narrative is further interrupted by episodes focalized through Raka's own perspective, in which her alterity is fully revealed. Raka is drawn as an Indian version of l'enfant sauvage in her seeming ability to roam wild and apparently unconcerned by physical discomfort and even pain. The flora and fauna of the Kasauli hills appear vividly in the descriptions from her point of view, but the infrequency of free indirect style keeps her interiority hidden. Silent and withdrawn in company, she does not respond to Nanda's overtures, and seems to inhabit a world outside of the realm of everyday language as much as the language of interiority. In emerging into Nanda's consciousness, Raka, as a conscious subject, however, remains unspoken in the text, a strategy which augments the construct of her as the Imaginary.

But the text goes on to deconstruct Raka's alterity as sign of her liberation from the symbolic order of the father. In chapter 11, she appears as the voyeur looking in on a scene in the ballroom of the Kasauli clubhouse; she was told by Ram Lal, Nanda's cook and housekeeper, that there might be a fancy-dress ball. The description of the ball, mediated by her perspective, is a prolonged nightmare in which the revellers in their disguise metamorphose into half-human, half-bestial creatures of lunatic frenzy, and their antics into scenes of bloodshed, mutilation, decapitation. The shocking violence in Raka's transformation of the scene points to that hidden trauma which belies her apparent self-completion, and shows how mistaken Nanda is in her observations of her great-grandchild. Unable to bear the scene she is watching, Raka flees in extreme distress while 'All the caged, clawed, tailed, headless male and female monsters followed her, pell-mell...' (FM 71). In the passage that comes immediately following, we can see the text's crucial disclosure:

> Somewhere behind them, behind it all, was her father, home from a party, stumbling and crashing through the curtains of night, his mouth opening to let out a flood of rotten stench, beating at her mother with hammers and fists of abuse – harsh, filthy abuse that make Raka cower under her bedclothes and wet the mattress in fright, feeling the stream of urine warm and weakening between her legs like a stream of blood, and her mother lay down on the floor and shut her eyes and wept. Under her feet, in the dark, Raka felt that flat, wet jelly of her mother's being squelching and quivering, so that she didn't know where to put her feet and wept as she tried to get free of it. Ahead of her, no longer on the ground but at some distance now, her mother was crying. Then it was a jackal crying. (FM 71–2)

Inscribed in this unspeakable version of the primal scene, now conjured by memory, is the self-violation inflicted on Raka through witnessing paternal violence. She is hidden from view, protecting herself from the ravages of the symbolic order in the kinetic language of abuse, and shuns but cannot reject the maternal body on which the symbolic order is writ large. The 'crying' of the mother is not forgotten; although the child has no language to describe their shared – but also separate – experience of violence and violation, and can hardly comprehend the full horror of what she has witnessed, she is traumatized and haunted by the mother's helplessness as much as by the father's brutality.

To Nanda, Raka is alterity, enviable and exemplary in her autonomy and self-completeness. What she cannot see is that, for Raka, memory is a madhouse and it can act to disfigure present reality, and incorporate it – as it does the ballroom scene – into past madness. Raka's wildness, and her seeming ability to merge into the wilderness of Kasauli, is an illusion of freedom; as the text shows, at this moment and in chapters where the third-person narrative perspective focuses on Raka and is focalized through her, her wildness is the sign of a disordered self, the havoc wrought on her in the madhouse of memory. To the reader, Nanda's efforts to draw Raka closer to her are fraught with danger; she not only runs the risk of breaking her isolation – as she herself appreciates but interprets as a positive change – but is treading, without being aware of doing so, on the precarious border between the prison-house of memory and the madhouse of memory.

In order to engage Raka's attention, to draw her great-granddaughter into her own past, and so to create in Raka those feelings of kinship reviving in herself, Nanda spins a tale of her own childhood in Kashmir, a landscape of snow, water, and fecundity, the geographical other of arid Kasauli. The story, begun at the dinner table, is in a succession of episodes, each told for as long as they hold Raka's attention, and a new one begun the moment she shows signs of restiveness, and each more fantastical than the one before. In the stories, Nanda's own father is gardener, producing fruits for the family, and zoo-keeper whose wild animals share the dinner table and cling to humans in affection. Nanda, succeeding her father, talks of herself as the keeper of unusual and exotic animals, and furthermore, about her rides in the moonlight of Kashmir. The stories circle round the figure of the father in the feminization of a lineage – *patria* into *matria* – of which Nanda is an earlier and Raka the latest arrival, and in which Nanda's husband – Raka's great-grandfather – is either marginalized or transformed into benevolence. 'Home', in the fairy-tale of the past, is where life in the wilderness comes inside, not to be domesticated and devitalized, but rather to become kith and kin in the very act of everyday life. This kinship between nature and human culture, or between the wild and the tamed, breaks through the symbolic attribution of domestic routine to the 'cuckoo's song', an earlier move which suggests nature being co-opted by human memory rather than reimagined in a primordial bond with humankind. The stories exemplify memory as confabulation, the memory of desire, oriented in one direction towards remaking the past and in another, towards a future freed because it can be made different from the past. Not surprisingly, the book which Nanda has been reading up to this point is *The Travels of Marco Polo*, a journey into the exotic remembered, displacing the world of ordered nature in *The Pillow Book of Sei Shonagon*.

Nanda's stories fail to produce the desired effect upon Raka, and this attempt at kinship is shown to rebound upon Nanda as she is confronted both with the falsehood of her own story, and its practice of deceit:

> She thought of how she had filled, not this house but the other, earlier ones, for Raka's amusement – with furniture, treasures, trophies, even, dear God, with a zoo. She shrivelled up in her chair with horror at the thought and relaxed only when she recalled, with dignity, that she had not done that to Carignano. Even when at her most desperate to beguile Raka, she had not used, or misused, Carignano, for that shameful purpose. Carignano she had kept clean, true, open for the wind to blow through. (*FM* 104)

Drawing back from the brink, Nanda apprehends that her fairy-tale of *matria* is an effort at myth-making designed to tame and domesticate her great-granddaughter, and that, in so doing, she not only betrays Raka but connives in putting herself back into a past where family obligation overrode all demands of truth to the self and others, and enforced upon her a life of having to put up with her husband's infidelity and her marriage as a lie. If, as mother, Nanda is full of guilt about her own failure, here she recognizes her connivance in time, she thinks, not to repeat her earlier failure in her relations with Raka. Carignano is conceived as the space of the woman's self-creation grounded on memory's commitment to verity and truth against its power to fabricate, distort, and deceive. On the cusp of a creative flowering that would see the publication of her three most significant novels to date (*Clear Light of Day, In Custody, Baumgartner's Bombay*), Nanda's mental and emotional struggles in *Fire on the Mountain* can be read as a mnemonic of Desai's own strenuous reflexivity about the woman seeking to re-create her self in a process where she must necessarily both remember and reimagine her past. For Desai, this process is inseparable from the trials of creating herself in art where, like Nanda, she has to work with and against memory, simultaneously turning to it for the resources of self and creativity, to remain truthful to what is remembered, and yet fighting the issue of this truth in obsession and trauma.

In the final section of the novel the three women are joined in their separate tragedies. The arrival of Illa Das at Carignano confronts Nanda with the full significance of her own practice of fantasy on Raka. In the lonely, mean, impoverished, and endangered life that Illa Das is forced into, the uses of memory offer a precarious means of salvaging a sense of self-esteem, and of claiming the attention, no matter how attenuated, of society. At tea, Illa's voice, in unbearable pitch, speaks interminably of the past, and to Nanda, who is forced to listen, it is 'a voice no human being ought to have had: it was anti-social to possess' (*FM* 5). The unbridgeable distance between this 'anti-social' voice and what it speaks of sharpens the pathos of Illa. Her account, re-membered in nostalgia, of the past life of Nanda's household as a rich social tapestry, full of human warmth and the pleasures and satisfaction of good company and conversation, is crucial to Illa's self-worth – that she too has once experienced life in its plenitude. Nanda, behind apparent composure, is increasingly perturbed not only by Illa's fantasy of her self and Nanda's family history, but more fundamentally by the dissociation between memory and truth which enables Illa's account and which bonds Illa to her in feelings of admiration and loyalty.

On her way home from Carignano, Illa Das is raped and strangled by the farmer whose daughter she is trying to protect from a forced marriage. As Nanda hears the news over the phone, the text shows how, in a rush of epiphanic discovery, she recognizes the falsehoods which shape and haunt her: her own lies to Raka, her husband's, and Illa's. In the final moment, the text suggests her suicide – 'Nanda Kaul on the stool with her head hanging, the black telephone hanging, the long wire dangling' (*FM* 145) – which is glimpsed through the window by Raka, herself in a final act of witnessing, who has come to tell her great-grandmother that she has set fire to the forest in the ravine below Carignano. The melodrama of this ending is palpable, and speaks of the collapse of the façade of dignity and composure which Nanda has struggled to maintain all her life.[7] She sees the truth of her self-fabrications precisely at the moment of her self-annihilation; the wildness of liberation she so desires is made present in the fire of destruction.

While memory is an agent of recall and retrieval of the past, in the stories which Nanda and Illa tell about themselves, memory is also made possible by the process of narrative, so that the women's self-identities in time are thrown open to the transactions between fact and the factitious as they shift and change throughout the text. Memory in narrative and as narrative implements the human drive towards wholeness, both of the self and in its relations with others, and while Desai shows a full recognition of the work of memory in self-construction and self-creation, she also subjects it to an ethical scrutiny which discriminates between the seductions of falsehood and the commitment to truth. The fate of both Nanda and Illa exposes the perils of false memory, as deliberate fabrication in Nanda's case or self-delusion in Illa's, and Nanda's suicide is the moment, resonant with tragic irony, when she acknowledges that there is no possibility of wholeness without responsibility to the past as the truth of fact. Desai is sympathetic to the woman's desire for the created self, but her judgement, as a realist, is severe on woman's complicity with a compromised sense of reality that perpetuates falsehood in the name of reparation of a historical wounding to the self. In this respect, *Fire on the Mountain* is consistent with the indictments of Indian woman's secret connivance that we have seen in the article mentioned earlier.

This is an issue which returns in *Clear Light of Day*, a novel in which Desai explores in much more nuanced detail the work of memory, and, from a different vantage, suggests 'the truth that the past is now inscribed within the present not only as curse, injury, and disfigurement but also as material for what is potentially, but far from assuredly, a different future'.[8] *Clear*

Light of Day also develops with great subtlety the references of private histories to public events which *Fire on the Mountain* only manages to point to in the colonial and post-independence history of Carignano. Writing appreciatively of Salman Rushdie's *Midnight's Children*, Desai appraises how, to Rushdie, 'if individual history does not make much sense unless seen against the national background, nor does national history make sense unless seen in the form of individual lives and histories'.[9] 'India', as a semantic project in *Clear Light of Day*, published a year before *Midnight's Children*, exemplifies the interaction between 'national' and 'individual' histories as much as does Rushdie's novel. As Shirley Chew observes, the novel shows a 'passionate commitment' on the part of Desai to remake the past in order to give women a voice in the 'motherland'.[10]

At first sight, *Clear Light of Day* postulates a binary, and oppositional, relation between past and present. Bim, who remains behind in the family home to look after her alcoholic aunt and mentally disabled brother, is contrasted with Tara, her younger sister, who marries a diplomat and travels and lives abroad; Tara seems mobile, capable of leaving the past while Bim stagnates; the family home in Old Delhi is the place of fading gentility, while New Delhi is progress and modernity. In this series of binary opposites, history is construed as disjunct temporalities in which the events of Independence and Partition are closed episodes untraced and untraceable in postcolonial everyday life. These superficial impressions of the past and present as binary opposites are challenged by the very structure of the narrative, which does not follow a linear pattern, and, in this respect, points unmistakably to the refusal of memory to abide by the order of time and the discipline of individual self-construction. In Freud, memory is both recall and the outcome of remembering in narrative, and, hence, subject to the interpretation and reinterpretation of the subject who remembers, and open to the interpretation of the analyst. *Clear Light of Day* is haunted by a third aspect of Freud's speculations on memory: its return in the uncanny which, even as it exists alongside his causal and positivistic account of the self in the past and present, also problematizes the assumptions of temporal sequencing which this account belies. In liberating memory from such sequencing, the novel explores its range of possibilities in the forming of the self in history: to sequester or bind individuals to their past so that individual histories take shape as narratives of determinism; to enable changing re-presentations of the past, or what Walter Benjamin calls 'the capacity for endless interpolations into what has been';[11] to foster the transformations and renewals of self and social relations which re-presentation brings. The characters in *Clear Light of Day* revisit their own pasts in order better to comprehend the truth about themselves and their relations with each other, and it is precisely this appeal to truth which underwrites memory's unpredictability, and orients its mobile energies towards the reparations of the self and history.

In the novel's opening chapter, Tara has come home on a holiday visit, and the return is the occasion for memory to throw up the sisters' agreements and disagreements about how they see themselves, each other, and the past they share. At this starting point in the narrative, memory is triggered off or targets the smallest details of observation or experience as the sisters struggle to settle down to their reunion. To Bim, Tara appears brisk and confident, very different from the 'languid little girl' she remembers (*CLD* 10), while Tara partly wishes to sink 'languidly down into the passive pleasure of having returned to the familiar' and partly resents the fact that Bim has allowed 'nothing to change' (*CLD* 12). At moments, their reunion seems a re-enactment of childhood pleasure, a 'passage of lightness' (*CLD* 20); at others, it reminds both of the sharp discord and their separate experiences. Each also seems locked away in her own isolated remembrance, in the special horror of particular childhood moments they alone experience. Tara remembers witnessing her father pressing a syringe in her mother's arm

> so that she tilted her head back with a quick gasp of shock, or pain – Tara saw her chin rising up into the air and the grey head sinking back into the pillow and heard a long, whimpering sigh like an air-bag minutely punctured so that Tara had fled, trembling, because she was sure she had seen her father kill her mother.
>
> All her life Tara had experienced that fear – her father had killed her mother. (*CLD*, 22–3)

In invoking this primal scene, memory reminds Tara of her estrangement not only from home but also from herself, which belies the confidence that Bim notices. The two sisters also differ sharply in their remembrance of their past in relation to their brother, Raja. Tara's experience is one of her own exclusion from the closeness of her elder siblings; ironically, this memory of distance enables her to remain in contact with Raja and perform the rituals of family association in her annual visits to him which Bim rejects because her memory of their closeness inflects Raja's marriage and departure to Hyderabad as betrayal. In this light, Bim, who seems to be the one to have shouldered the care of the family Tara leaves behind, and the guardian of family continuity, reappears as someone unable to come to terms with the past. The full variety of memory's work, and the destabilizing effect of that work in the attempt by the self to comprehend itself and its relations with others informs the opening chapter.

From the temporality of the opening chapter, where memory conjures in the present the scattered and inchoate debris of time past, the text moves, in chapters 2 and 3, to narrate memory as it structures the sisters' and their family's histories. Bim and Tara cohere in their remembrance of childhood neglect by a diabetic mother too preoccupied with her own illness and diversions and a father totally absorbed by her needs. This negative bond of exclusion is given a positive turn in the children's shared intimacy with their widowed aunt Mira, herself an outcast who, after a life of misery in the marital home, is replaced among the needs and affection of the children. Memory structures the affective history of family as the dialectic of rejection and intimacy, displacement and relocation, but the children's experience is haunted by moments which cannot be folded back into the dialectic, which are no less important in defining their collective and individual selves, and yet elude linear organization and synthesized outcomes.

When their mother is removed to the hospital, and their father spends all his evenings away from home, parental absence is troubling but not regretted by the children. After her death which the children did not witness and the funeral they did not attend, the mother's departure is registered only in the sense of guilt the children share for not really being more upset that she is gone. They exchange 'looks of mutual guilt when the neighbours came and wept a few tears required by custom ... and tacitly agreed to keep their guilt a secret. The secret replaced their mother's presence in the house, a kind of ghostly surrogate which they never quite acknowledged and quite often forgot' (*CLD*, 54). This unspoken and unspeakable feeling which lurks on the margins of the children's collective consciousness is disinterred by the narratorial voice free of character focalization, and hence of subjective remembrance, and reinserts into family history as the history of emotions, a space for the operation of the unconscious.

The reader is reminded much more vividly of such operations especially in and through the figures of animals in the novel. Badshah, Bim's dog, barks 'in that magnificent voice that Bim admired so much and that soured – or spiced – her relations with the neighbours' (*CLD*, 6). Bim's preferred isolation, hinted at here through Badshah, is contrasted with Tara's encounter, narrated much later, with the mad dog which is trapped in the school latrine and shot. While her schoolmates scramble to look and exclaim at the blood, 'Tara did not see, kept her fingers pressed into her eyes till blue and red stars burst out of them, but she was aware that blood had been spilt and washed over her feet, warm and thick and living. Unlike Bim and Raja, she never pestered her parents for a dog' (*CLD* 128). Alone in her fear, Tara's isolation is of a nature and quality different from that which Bim prefers, and the difference cannot simply be explained as one which separates the child from the adult or innocence from maturity. The two incidents speak to each other in a dialogue that is outside the dialectic frame by pointing to how the sisters' shared experience of rejection is individuated in their unconscious selves. Tara's horror at the bloody death of the mad dog, and her inability to erase her misinterpretation of the scene earlier discussed where she sees her father giving her mother an injection, are consistent with each other in pointing to a narrative of the individual in family as the memory of the irruptions of the unspeakable, the unacknowledgeable, the phantasmagoric. If Aunt Mira's arrival and caring presence help replace the bonds of affection in the family and among the children themselves, she also embodies the despond and psychological malaise which haunt the children and their memories. Not long after her arrival, at her suggestion, Bim and Tara's mother agrees to buy a cow so that the children can have good-quality nourishment. For a while, the cow and its calf are a great success, warmly welcomed by the children as both provider and pet, until one night, it breaks free of its tether, and drowns in the family well:

> The well then contained death as it once had contained merely water, frogs and harmless floating things. The horror of that death by drowning lived in the area behind the carvanda hedge like a mad relation, a family scandal or a hereditary illness to re-emerge. It was a blot, a black sinking blot... Most horrifying of all, the calf pined and died. It kept Aunt Mira awake in the night and nightly she saw the white cow die in the black well. (*CLD* 107–8)

The well, hidden away and seldom referred to, is the narratorial sign of what is normally shunned by the children's conscious remembrance and the novel's realist discourse – an emptiness but also a space filled with inchoate feelings that reappear at moments when least expected. Years later, as Bim sits with Tara and her husband, Bakul, in the garden during their visit, the death of 'Mira-*masi*', which they have not spoken about – but which the reader knows about from prior narrative – is mentioned by Bim. 'Then they were all three silent', not because of a collective sense of regret at the death, but because the mentioning of it marks the moment which breaks the sociality that has sustained their company during the visit: 'They all sat together as if at the bottom of a well, caught by its stone walls, trapped in its gelatinous waters' (*CLD* 152). A moment of affiliation is also the moment when the family, haunted by the unhomeliness of decay and death, feels this affiliation as a common entrapment that cannot be spoken of, and from which they are unable to break free. The discourse of family in the text, as the outcome of memory's multiple constructions of history, is shot through with the ambivalence that Homi Bhabha observes of the nation: 'The other is never outside or beyond us; it emerges forcefully, within cultural discourse, when we *think* we speak most intimately and indigenously "between ourselves".'[12]

Bhabha's comments are also germane to the question of the family's uncertain location in community. At first, it seems that the distance between parents and children is replicated in the isolation of the family in community. The children's parents never had time for their neighbours, and the casual visitors to the house – men from the office, bridge-partners from the club – only emphasize the family's isolation. The Misra sisters and brothers who live next door are tolerated rather than liked, rarely mentioned in the childhood narrative, and the adult Bim finds the sisters' self-denial in order to support their brothers' idleness distasteful and distressing. But if the Misras are dysfunctional others against whom the family's own problematic affiliation defines its difference, in Raja's attachment to their Muslim landlord, Hyder Ali, memory reconnects the family's history – both its affiliation and separation in time – to the larger history of the Partition, and the dislocation of family to the separatist dynamic that orients, or disorients, the early history of the Indian nation.

As a child, Raja has always been fascinated by Hyder Ali's household, a fascination premised not so much on its material well-being as on the bounty of its cultural capital. The Ali family compound is the meeting place of old Delhi society, frequented nightly by writers, singers, artists, and men of distinction who enjoy their host's informal but gracious hospitality. Before actually meeting Hyder Ali, Raja is already 'dazzled by the impressive figure of the old gentleman with silvery hair, dressed in white riding clothes and seated upon the white horse that Raja had for years envied him' (*CLD* 7). Raja's fascination expresses itself through his absorption in Urdu language and poetry, against which Hindi, 'in its modern, clipped, workaday form' (*CLD* 47), appears to him dull and plebeian. Throughout his childhood and into adolescence, he cultivates a self-identity in Urdu, spends long hours reading in Hyder Ali's private library, attends the evening sessions of Urdu poetry and song in the company of Hyder Ali's Muslim friends, and despite his father's irritation, decides that his chosen career would be that of a Muslim scholar. In Raja, Desai embodies her own memories of pre-Partition India, where cultural self-identity resists containment within ethnic and communalist boundaries, and, as a sign of agency, is open to individual choice and adoption. Writing of the memoirs of Partition, Urvashi Butalia has observed that the generalities of large-scale events and statistics exist 'publicly in books. [But] [t]he particular is harder to discover; it exists privately in the stories told and retold inside so many households in India and Pakistan.'[13] Raja's story in *Clear Light of Day*, and its place in the history of his family, is Partition remembered as private history, an elegiac conjuration of lost realities, and also a remembrance, through a narrative of ambivalent family loyalty and disaffiliation, of the public memory of convulsion and catastrophic rupture.

Raja's attachment to Hyder Ali and Urdu speaks of romance and romantic desire, the other sign of which is his fondness for English Romantic verse, especially that of Byron, which he intersperses with Urdu poetry in his reading and his recitations to Bim. Bim, whose closeness to Raja excludes Tara, is, in turn, left behind as Raja turns away from Hindi and family to an alien language, and a cultural and masculine other – both a quasi-father figure and male society – with whom she can feel no identification. The momentum of Raja's turn is temporarily arrested when he contracts tuberculosis and falls ill, at the very point in the public history when the reality of Partition begins to take hold of the community, and their Muslim neighbours start disappearing. Raja is reduced to a passive and agentless, and frequently debilitated, onlooker as his desired cultural other is fragmented and dislocated. In becoming ill, he is reincorporated into the spirit of his family so long overshadowed by the illness of his mother, and refeminized, not only through his symbolic inheritance of his mother's disability, but also in his total dependence on Bim's care. It is Bim who sponges his forehead, wipes the sweat from his face, and runs up and down between the rooftop where she watches the city, Delhi, in flames from a distance, and the sick room where Raja, his face 'bloodless, fine and drawn' (CLD 44), tosses and turns in anxiety and frustration. 'His situation', defined by Bim's female gaze,

> was Romantic in the extreme, Bim could see as she ... helped him struggle out of one muslin shirt and into another – his heavy, limp body as she lifted it as spent and sapped as a bled fish, and the city of Delhi burning down about them. He hoped, like Byron, to go to the rescue of those in peril. Instead, like Byron, he lay ill, dying, Bim was sure he was dying. (CLD 60)

Circumscribing Raja in her female gaze, Bim is also circumscribed by what she can see or what her desire to return Raja to herself and the family disables her from seeing. Raja's romanticism develops a much more muscular edge as his strength recovers, and as Bim's attention is distracted by Aunt Mira's alcoholic delirium after their mother's death. As the responsibility of care for both her aunt and Baba increasingly defines Bim's place in the family, Raja retreats from the forefront of her attention, and the text itself. There are occasional references to his correspondence with Hyder Ali's family which has resettled in Hyderabad, and the Urdu verses Raja composes and sends to them, but his decision to depart for Hyderabad after Aunt Mira's death is presented to Bim as a fact which she can only accept. When he confronts Bim with his decision, Raja

> shouted 'I have to go. Now I can go. I have to begin my life some time, don't I? You don't want me to spend all my life down in this hole, do you? You don't think I can go on living just to keep my brother and sister company, do you?'
> 'I never said a word,' said Bim coldly. (*CLD* 100)

There is a deliberate ambivalence in the text about whether this decision is an entirely private one, made in the interest of the self, and in the name of self-development, or whether it articulates the recalcitrance of the individual will in the face of the enforced segregation between Hindu and Muslim communities, which is the public outcome of the Partition. To Bim, it is an entirely private decision, an abandonment of family and responsibility, and not a political act. The text is silent on what Raja's motives might have been, or what they might have been in retrospect; his future is not narrated at first hand or directly, but mediated by Tara's report of visiting him and his family, after his marriage to Hyder Ali's daughter in Hyderabad. In this ambivalence, and in the parting of Raja and Bim, what the text shows is Partition not only as the moment of rupture which is differently played out in individual lives and families, but also as an event whose meanings have not been fully grasped or understood by those on whom it has consequential impact, and may elude them still.

Equally ambivalent is how to frame Bim's own experience in public history. Her single romantic encounter in the novel is the courtship of Mr Biswas, which happens during the time of Aunt Mira's progressive alcoholism. As she listens, on the way home from a concert, to his account of his student days in Germany, she remarks on how lucky he is to have known 'such glories – such joys', although she feels no real interest in his story, unlike Tara and Raja who succumb to the promise of what lies outside the family. Through the window of the bus, she sees the city walls and the massed jungle of rag-and-tin huts that had grown beneath them, housing the millions of refugees who were struggling in across the new border... They swarmed and crawled with a kind of crippled, subterranean life that made Bim feel that the city would never recover from this horror, that it would be changed irremediably, that it was already changed, no longer the city she had been born in. She set her jaw and stared into its shadowy thickness, wretched with its wretchedness. (*CLD* 86)

Just as it is impossible to disentangle the private and public meanings of Raja's act of departure, the text is again characteristically discreet about the complex psychology that interweaves Bim's emotions about an unsatisfactory courtship, her anxieties about Mira's feverish condition, and the 'horror' of a city convulsed by the Partition, overrun by 'crippled, subterranean life'. Bim's meetings with Mr Biswas come to an end after she visits his house to meet his mother, and realizes the querulous demands and drudgery which await her as a prospective daughter-in-law. Out on the streets, with him lamely beside her, she hears the news of Gandhi's assassination, and while he begins 'to sway from side to side in ritual mourning', she runs away from him, thinking 'only of rushing to Raja with the news' (*CLD* 93). The moment when she rejects Mr Biswas is inextricable from the momentous event of the assassination and her immediate response which seems to be oriented not by a sense of national tragedy but by the urgent – and understandable – need to establish contact with family and those to whom she feels closest.

As the text remembers these episodes in Bim's personal and family history, it also situates the political traumas of the new Indian nation in a narrative of affect that involves the nation's most ordinary citizens. Writing recently in the context of a review of Mohsin Hamid's *Moth Smoke*, Desai says, '[after Partition], time has not stood still... In fact, things hardly ceased to happen: life was chaotic, dramatic, and traumatic at every hour, in every city and village and house'.[14] Public history, which aggregates individuals as an anomalous collective and positions them as respondents rather than agents, is displaced, and its integrative dynamic is dispersed so that the emotional history of the Partition and the assassination is returned, through narrative reconfiguration, as the hybrid space of the private and the public, the individualized and the intersubjective, will and determination. As the woman who rejects the traditional roles of wife and daughter-in-law and yet shoulders the responsibility of family care and custody, Bim is the ambivalent sign of the text's reinscription of hybridity within the history of the nation's women.

In the final chapter, *Clear Light of Day* draws to a close in the present as memory and narrative connect present with past in a network of causalities from which the sisters both emerge and against which they struggle. In this final move to conceptualize memory as causality, past experience is reinterpreted, mobilized, and develops new or different meanings. Tara now sees her marriage for what it is: an escape from parental neglect, and, more importantly, an individuating act of release from the family malaise symptomized by her mother's long-term illness and Mira's madness. Her admission, 'I didn't think of it that way then,' (*CLD* 156), is the paradigmatic speech act of memory: a past experience is retrieved and, in this retrieval, a new interpretation is proposed which makes a different sense of the experience and hence, an alternative causality. In knowing the past differently, self-identity is renewed. The creative work of memory which is premised on the imperative of truth – the desire to know what one's actions really mean in order to locate oneself as realistically and truthfully as possible in the present – this is the clear light of day.

To struggle through the shadows and spectral spaces haunted by the ghosts of the past, and to reach the clear light of day requires heroic effort from Bim – heroism of a different order from what she has shown in taking up the burden of the family. For so long, she has appeared taciturn and in control, silent about her anger and hurt at Raja's departure, and inarticulate about the depth of her love for him, Tara, and Baba. Despite Tara's promptings, she cannot bring herself to agree to visit Raja and his wife, and her sudden admission to Tara that she has always felt she will 'end up in that well ... one day' leaves Tara floundering, unsure of what Bim is disclosing about herself. As in the past, the sisters, in their movement towards self-renewal and reaffiliation are both identical and separate. Withdrawing to the silence of her own room, Bim admits the truth of her profound love in its imperfection 'because it had flaws and inadequacies and did not extend to all equally' (*CLD* 165), and the need therefore to be forgiving of others and be forgiven. Like Nanda Kaul in *Fire on the Mountain*, Bim is the woman rejected, isolated, and isolating in her carefully maintained façade of uncaring.

Clear Light of Day, as critics have pointed out, breaks through to show the possibility of her reconciliation with self and others, and replacement in community, in what Shirley Chew has called a 'visionary ending'. However, to Chew, this ending 'can only encompass without resolving the violence that lies unredeemable at [the novel's] core, and which is embodied in the tragic figure of Aunt Mira'.[15] There is also another haunting which has so far escaped critical attention. In a moment which recalls the ending of 'The Farewell Party', Bim, after Tara's departure to Hyderabad, joins the Misra sisters and brothers in an evening gathering of song and music, together with other guests who have 'come out of the steamy city to the cool dark lawn in Old Delhi to listen to a little music under the dusty stars' (*CLD* 177). The setting, scene, and action recall the lost culture of Hyder Ali's household and, in the pleasure of the present community, this memory runs as the subterranean current of another community's displacement and exile, and the nation's fractured legacy.

3

Comic Man, Tragic Man

Anxious and sullen, Deven, the protagonist of *In Custody*, is to all appearances as unmemorable as the town Mirpore in which he lives. Inhabited mainly by petty tradesmen, Mirpore is one among the many populous but nondescript provincial outposts littering the dry dusty crossroads of the northern Indian plains. It has no history to speak of, no distinguished landmarks; its reason for existence, rather like Deven's, is a mystery. If Mirpore can be said to have a focus at all, it resides in what the narrator calls an 'addiction to total dehydration' (*IC* 15). Deven's life as a teacher of Hindi literature in the inadequately resourced and academically suspect Lala Ram Lal College is as arid as the town itself, punctuated occasionally by bouts of humiliation when his ineptitude in the classroom is greeted by the students' derisory laughter. Like Mirpore which has no historical or cultural significance and where the infrastructure is poorly built and shoddily maintained, Deven has a minimal support system in his work and family, and survives the everyday in a state of need rather than actual material privation.

But, unlike Mirpore, he has a hidden centre, an inner resource which sustains him in his otherwise desiccated existence. He harbours a passion, well hidden from college, for Urdu poetry, especially the work of Nur, the once illustrious poet whose time, as the novel is to show, is well past. In this passion is embedded Deven's desire for an alternative world; in the novel, the verdant symbolism and lush romantic landscapes of Urdu lyric are pointedly contrasted with the aridity of Mirpore and his monotonous life. This passion is mapped onto the seduction which the metropolis holds for the small-town dweller – a classic third-world trajectory which Desai has earlier plotted in narrating the tensions between the rural and the urban in *The Village by the Sea*. To Deven, Delhi, where Nur lives, is 'the capital with its lost treasures of friendships, entertainment, attractions and opportunities'; between Mirpore and Delhi is an 'impassable desert' that has turned into a 'no-man's land that lies around a prison' (*IC* 18) where Deven is incarcerated by ennui and the growing and debilitating realization that life for him holds nothing but disappointment. With characteristic deftness, Desai mobilizes the representation of the Indian location – its geography of city and strung-out provincial towns – so that it points symbolically towards Deven's self-identity on the one hand – or what Desai calls the 'drawing of a landscape which is also an inscape'[1] – and the historical and social frames of his existence on the other.

Deven's subjectivity is further seen in his engagement with the other college staff and the students, and his wife and son. Or perhaps the lack of engagement would be more accurate although what emerges from the narrative is that in their cohabitation of a similar existential milieu, they share a common fate which is not of their own choosing, and which they are powerless to change. On an annual college holiday, the staff 'hung round the corridors, not knowing quite what to do with themselves', while the students who remain loiter around discussing 'that something better to do that they did not have' (*IC* 98). This collective loss of purpose is emphasized in the garden party – intertextual with Bina's – in which the rituals of tea-drinking and small-talk dominate, and where the staff, Deven among them, measure constantly and anxiously their proximity to and distance from the Principal. As teacher, Deven is neither respected nor listened to; as a member of staff, he is hardly more noticeable to those as lowly placed as himself, and certainly unnoticed by those further up the institutional hierarchy. The college pays him a meagre salary and holds over him the threat of dismissal, and in so doing, ensures his servility.

Marginal to the college and college life, Deven's antipathy to his wife, Sarla, and distance from their son, Manu, constitute once again, a narrative of family dysfunction. Like Harish's wife in *Surface Textures*, Sarla is preoccupied with the stringencies of a tight family budget, and can barely conceal her resentment against a husband who, in her eyes, has failed to provide. *In Custody*, however, invests Sarla's discontent with a history by tracing it briefly to her expectations as a young woman before marriage, and subsequent disappointments. Sarla exemplifies the woman who, unlike the type referred to in 'A Secret Connivance' but also in some ways her counterpart, has interiorized the glossy advertising images of the modern Indian household, and fabricated a self-identity which she expects to be realized through marriage. The husband is, of course, the significant other in this, the one who in Sarla's mind, will be the conniver in her desire, and the agent of its fulfilment. In a marriage where she confronts daily 'the thwarting of her anticipations' (*IC* 68), Sarla has come to blame Deven for all her disappointments in life. What the narrative shows is that though bonded in a common fate as victims of life's betrayal, they have no empathy for each other. Each looks elsewhere for an alternative, but while 'at least Deven had his poetry', 'she had nothing, and so there was an added accusation and bitterness in her look' (*IC* 68). In only one episode in the novel is Deven shown deriving some comfort and content from family life, and that is when he takes his son Manu out for a walk after he returns from his escapade to Delhi and the derangement of his encounter with Nur and his household. This interlude when father and son strike up an unfamiliar bond is a luminous moment in the text or, in the words of the narrator, a 'brief halcyon passage' (*IC* 74) which quickly comes to a close as they arrive home to be greeted by a cynical Sarla handing Deven a letter from Nur with its fatal summons to revisit Delhi. Deven 'knew his doom had searched him out and found him after all' (*IC* 74).

Before turning to the relationship between Deven and Nur which is central to the text, it is interesting to look at some of Desai's comments about *In Custody* and to consider their significance and implications in our reading of the text. So far what we have seen of the novel – the dismal lives of its characters, their powerlessness to defy or change what fate seems to have laid down for them – argues a strong tragic orientation, and yet, in the interview with Kirsten Holst Petersen, Desai observes that 'the book was a comedy' and elaborates:

> There is an order of comedy that makes you laugh in order not to cry ... It is not meant to be jolly laughter, companionable laughter; it is bitter, rueful laughter. That seems to me the best answer you can make to the world the way it is.[2]

It is not immediately clear from the quotation whether 'you' refers to Desai herself, Deven, or the reader drawn into his hapless life. There are few instances in the novel of Deven finding either his life or those of others comic and laughable. But if the 'you' refers to an authorial perspective, then it provides a clue to understanding Desai's delicate balancing act between satire and sympathy in representing Deven, and the comic-tragic ambivalence of the novel itself. There *is* something comical about the representation of the awkward little man who has 'never found a way to reconcile the meanness of his physical existence with the purity and immensity of his literary yearnings' (*IC* 19–20). An inflated sense of self, often unrecognized by the character who suffers from it, is a conventional target of satire, but in relation to Deven, this satiric tenor is complicated, tempered, and distracted by the suggestion, in this quotation and also elsewhere in the text, that he at least recognizes the gap between reality and aspiration that is his life.

At the same time, if the reader is prompted into laughing at Deven's mean little existence, she is also made to feel the meanness of her own laughter. In embroiling himself in the project of interviewing Nur and recording the poet's voice for posterity, Deven is gulled and exploited by his childhood friend Murad, whose motives for plunging him repeatedly into embarrassment are not really explained in the text. The relationship between the two is something they are shown to be habituated to in their long acquaintance, and is variously represented as that between the bullying and the timid, the Falstaffian and the *ingenu*. In laughing at Deven, the reader is implicitly aligned with Murad; it is a laughter which greets the pathetic helplessness of the gull in conventional English satire. There is little doubt that Deven is gullible, but, unlike Murad, he is illuminated from within by a self-consciousness of his own inadequacies which none of the characters – least of all the great Nur – is capable of. Although this makes him socially inhibited and graceless, it is precisely this capacity to know what he is, and above all, what he is not, that transforms his meanness into a humility which turns the tables on the reader's laughter.

Deven's central weakness, the one which defines him, and which also paradoxically gives him the greatest dignity, is his love of Nur's poetry. The lover, as Shakespeare said in comic mood, is mad, and, in his madness, ridiculous to the eyes of the world and, indeed, to himself. But the love itself is bracketed from ridicule in the novel: as an experience of sensation, it is embodied in the voice of Deven's father reciting Nur's poem to him as a child, and as Deven himself recites the poem to Nur on his first visit to the poet, his own voice merges into the memory of his father's, and conjures the tenderness of childhood and warmth of paternal love (*IC* 40). Nur's poetry is treasured by Deven for its power to lift him out of time so that the past returns as familiar country to offer respite from the present, and the present can be transformed in the light of the past. In this reconfiguration of time, Deven, secured by love and in his love, undergoes a kind of metamorphosis. In the following passage, he continues to recite to Nur:

> A tender, almost feminine lilt entered his voice with those memories and the poet listened engrossed, now and then joining in with his own cracked voice as if he had forgotten the lines and was happy to be reminded ... As he continued, he began to be overcome by the curious sensation that he was his own mother, rocking back and forth on her heels as she half-sang, half-recited a story in the night, and that the white bolster-like figure on the bed beside him was a child, his child, whom he was lulling to sleep. He understood completely, in these minutes, how it must feel to be a mother, a woman. He had not known before such intimacy, such intense closeness as existed in that dark and shaded room where his voice merged with those of the pigeons to soothe the listening, lulled figure before him. He was also aware ... that this moment that contained such perfection of feeling, unblemished and immaculate, could not last, must break and disperse. (*IC* 41)

The astringent laughter of satire is temporarily displaced by the lyrical and regenerative impulse of romantic comedy, conventionally symbolized by the return or rebirth of the female principle in one or several of its social embodiments: as mother or daughter, wife or mistress. Here, the impulse is awakened in Deven, and acts as the psychical counterweight to his previously exclusive identification with the father, so that he becomes a perfect and complete whole in himself as both the source – male and female – and progeny of life. In this process, his customary self-consciousness of inadequacy is superseded; Nur is transformed into the child whom he can care for rather than be overawed by, and in his new understanding of what it is like to be a woman and mother, the self not only completes itself but also extends into the other. It is a moment out of time, of security, wholeness, and peace, but it is also a mark of Deven's intelligence that he is all too aware of its transience. In this awareness, Deven moves out of the novel's comic world – conceived as satiric and romantic – into the tragic realm, *sub specie aeternitatis*, of the mutable and deterministic.

In many ways, Nur is also situated in the undecidability of past and present, brilliance and loss, comedy and tragedy. He is the novel's chief figure of satiric ridicule – fat, importunate, infantalized, both *senex* and clown. The narrative, often focalized through Deven, returns time and again to representations of Nur's body and its dysfunctions: he complains about his piles, spits frequently into a spittoon, and in a scene which nearly maddens Deven, vomits in his second wife Imtiaz's bedroom after a drinking bout. He presides over his household like a lord of misrule, while his followers, whom Deven at first thought of as lovers of poetry, appear as disordered as him, swarming round like parasites who feed on his gluttonous body. Nur is constantly calling out for food – '*biryani* ... kebabs, kofta and dal' – and when it arrives, plunges his hand and lowers his face into it, lifting 'handfuls to his mouth from where it dropped or leaked on to his lap' (*IC* 48). He is both petulant child and the body in decay, poetic genius and a sick and wounded beast. In the earlier moment when he recites his poem with Deven, he appears as the father-substitute, the perfect embodiment of Deven's desire. Most of the time in the novel, his encounters with Deven drive the latter to extreme bewilderment, disillusionment, and near despair.

Deven's road out of Mirpore, both literally and metaphorically, is through the project, initiated by the callous Murad, of interviewing Nur and recording his voice for posterity. It begins and progresses as a series of mishaps that threaten to ruin his livelihood and deprive him of whatever minimal security his college post and family have so far offered. But even after his first disastrous visit to Delhi, when he encounters Nur's household, and is distraught at the disjunction between Nur as man and husband and Nur the poet, Deven is drawn back again and again to renew their contact. There is a double dynamic at work in the narrative of the relation between Deven and Nur: the irresistible bond of poetry itself and Deven's refusal, against all evidence of Nur's decline, to surrender to the vicissitudes of existence that challenge his love and belief in the pulchritude of Nur's creativity. In a number of moments in the novel, Deven is shown to be frustrated to the point of despair by the many delays to his project caused by the lack of funds, the incompetence of the young man, Chiku, who is supposed to help him with the recording, and the sheer unpredictability of Nur himself. It is also precisely at these moments that the narrator, consistent in her representation of Nur's changeability, suddenly offers the reader another vantage on the poet. At times when it seems that the recording could not continue any longer, Nur would 'open out one of his child's copy books on his knees and begin to read in a voice that was sing-song yet powerful' (*IC* 170), and speak to Deven about the context of the particular verse, its ideas and images, and the literary models he admires. It is these rare moments which redeem the enterprise for Deven, and, as far as he is concerned, rescue it from total futility.

In the novel, Nur's greatness as poet is embodied in recurrent descriptions of his voice which contrasts with the raucousness of his followers on the one hand and Deven's inarticulateness on the other. A third, gendered aspect of this contrast is with Imtiaz's solo performance of her own verse which is largely observed from Deven's point of view. Already shocked by her seemingly callous treatment of the sick Nur, Deven is scathing about her 'sad, wilted voice', which 'was as plain as her appearance' (*IC* 87).[3] In this reaction, and in his marriage with Sarla, the narrative points at Deven's troubled masculinity which disables empathy with women whose domestic unhappiness is ironically very like his own. It counterpoints also his assumption of the maternal and female roles we have seen in the quotation on page 47 which seems to suggest an ability to cross the gender divide. The dialogue between the comic-satiric and tragic discourses constitutes the intersubjective relations of the characters which, in turn, fuel the dynamic of the narrative of *In Custody*.

Grounding the relations between poetry, aesthetic truth, and mortality is the fate of Urdu, as language and culture, in post-independence India. In loving Nur's verse, Deven has aligned himself with decline, not only of the poet, but of Urdu itself in the novel's linguistic politics in which Hindi is represented as hegemonous. It is the disappearing venues for publishing Urdu verse and scholarship which make Murad's idea for immortalizing Nur's voice and verse so seductive to Deven. The consciousness of Urdu as a doomed language is shared by Nur himself, and contributes to his tragic sense of loss that counterbalances the satire on his corpulent and dysfunctional body. It is also evident in the insignificance of the language in the curriculum of Lala Ram Lal College and the marginalized position of the head of the Urdu department, Abid Siddiqui, whom Deven appeals to for help in asking the college for the funds to support his trips to Delhi and expenses for the interview. If Nur is the embodiment of Urdu's decay as the language of creativity, Siddiqui breathes the last gasps of serious Urdu scholarship. *In Custody* voices, much more resonantly than *Clear Light of Day*, Desai's elegiac lament of the doomed fate of Urdu in modern India, not only in its defeat by Hindi but also the loss of faith of its custodians – the incompetent buffoon Murad, Nur's decrepitude, and Siddiqui's final retreat. The spatial symbol of this fate is Siddiqui's crumbling house in Mirpore, once a grand mansion where night after night, his ancestors host performances of poetry and song attended by enthusiasts from the city. Siddiqui has survived among the broken masonry for many years but decides in the end to sell the house to a developer. During Deven's visit, Siddiqui describes for Deven a way of life and culture which the younger man apprehends as a kind of golden age. What Deven witnesses in Nur's house is the parnassian replay of a past which, instead of prelapsarian pleasure, becomes a nightmare of the fall that completely destabilizes his self-confidence and sanity.

The elegiac discourse on Urdu underlines Deven's belatedness. His love inspires a heroic leap of faith, not only into the unknown world of Nur and his household, but into the past itself in the belief that it can be preserved from oblivion and its memory secured for the future. Central to this is his assumed identity as the custodian of Nur's verse and memory – an assumption which begins on impulse rather than as a conscious act but which, in the course of the narrative, is shown to be naïve and self-delusory; so much so that the identity itself is time and again threatened with dissolution. At the nadir of his disillusionment with Nur and their disastrous encounters, Deven thinks of himself as 'a trapped animal' who has escaped the cage of his marriage and life only to 'blunder into another cage inhabited by some other trapped animal.' (IC 141–2) He thinks of himself as inheriting his father's weakness which made the latter 'an ineffectual, if harmless, teacher and householder ... [Deven] felt it inside him like an empty hole, one he had been staring at all his years, intimidated by its blackness and blankness' (IC 138). There is a sense of tragic determinism in his self-representation, which coordinates with the elegiac vantage on the doomed fate of Urdu language and culture.

At a moment near his death, Hugo Baumgartner, the protagonist of *Baumgartner's Bombay*, is to look at his life in the same way as Deven (*BB* 216). Or rather, Desai redeploys the image of the man looking into the abyss of his life to suggest the total emptiness that is his self-identity. The accidents of birth and history have estranged both Deven and Baumgartner from the languages and cultures of their location. But unlike Baumgartner, who will be discussed in detail in a moment, Deven develops consciousness about his situation vis-à-vis his fate and, consequently, agency. In many ways, Deven is Desai's modernist hero, the ordinary man placed on uncertain ground as the culture of his belonging fragments around him, and who gains stature and dignity as he fights its inevitable demise. If there is a tragic determinism in Desai's narrative vantage on the fate of Urdu language and culture, in Deven she embodies the redemption which a conscious acceptance and embrace of that fate can bring. As a grand record – or narrative – of Nur's greatness, Deven's project of recording, interview, and scholarly monograph has failed dismally. But in sifting through his memory of their encounters, he retrieves the rare moments when their voices resonate in harmony of recitation, and the bond, or 'alliance', between them that these moments implement. The bond is, as he realizes, also a constraint – 'if he was to be custodian of Nur's genius, then Nur would become his custodian and place him in custody too. This alliance could be considered an unendurable burden – or else a shining honour. Both demanded an equal strength' (IC, 225). Aspiration has been transformed, through trial, into the assured truth of the self's identity in a language and a culture; in this belonging, Deven's heroic stand against the tragedy of Urdu in modern India has a comic ending after all.

No such comic good fortune awaits Hugo Baumgartner as he makes his timid passage through the momentous events of twentieth-century history that would carry him from his birthplace in Berlin to a life of expatriation in Bombay. *Baumgartner's Bombay*, first published in 1988, is Desai's retrospective on the century. Though similar to *In Custody* and the other novels in its historical orientation, it crosses the boundaries between India and Europe, and through a fictional referencing of the tumultuous upheavals in Europe before and during the Second World War, shows how these upheavals in the imperial centre are played out in a distant location which is an outpost of empire. As we have seen in the interview cited in an earlier chapter, *Baumgartner's Bombay* is Desai's first attempt to remake in fiction the memory of her own German – and maternal – ancestry. It is also her first attempt at a world novel from two related postcolonial vantages: as a narrative of India in the dominant narrative discourse of the European experience of the Second World War, and of those dispossessed and culturally exiled by European history whose voices remain unheard in English-language fiction.

In himself and his life, Baumgartner exemplifies the tragic displacements suffered by large numbers of individuals in the last century, the unbelonging which haunts their everyday existence and estranges them wherever they are.[4] As a Jew, Baumgartner suffers a double displacement: from his native Germany, and from India, which serves at first as temporary refuge from Nazi persecution and eventually becomes his permanent abode. The narrative of *Baumgartner's Bombay* begins in the present, in postcolonial India at the moment after Baumgartner's death, and flashes back to his childhood in Germany before the Second World War. Time and place continue to shift backwards and forwards to spin a historical web that implicates the present as the legacy of the past. This is a narrative strategy – and a particular vantage on determinism in human history – which Desai has used to considerable effect in both *Clear Light of Day* and *In Custody*. But, unlike Bim and Deven who manage to elude the stranglehold of the past and transform it in the present, Baumgartner is dogged by the malignant legacies of his early history which he cannot, in the end, ignore or escape. Disaffiliated from German bourgeois culture by Nazi persecution, and unable to filiate with the cultures of his diasporic Indian location, Baumgartner's history is constituted of absence or loss, a process of being emptied of selfhood and cultural identity culminating in his murder and the oblivion of death. Against history, seen as callous, cruel, and tyrannical, Baumgartner is like a wounded animal, powerless and pitiable – Desai's tragic determinism is at its bleakest in *Baumgartner's Bombay*.

Deracinated and decultured, Baumgartner's extreme marginality is represented in the details of his quotidian experience and, significantly, as a loss of language. Of crucial importance in the narrative of his childhood is the introduction of German words, expressions, and quotations as material traces of Baumgartner's cultural origins. German is his first language, the language of his identity and cultural filiation. In the course of the novel, this Germanness, or what remains of it, is placed in relation to various language systems – Hebrew and the languages of India – which encode the values of the different cultures that Baumgartner encounters. The disharmonies that ensue are often rendered as miscommunication or an inability to communicate. Thus, Desai interweaves Baumgartner's German origins and his subsequent alienation from the cultures and societies he encounters.

Punctuating the narrative of his childhood are snatches of German songs, mostly nursery rhymes. Some of these songs would be specifically related to the context of his everyday life as, for example, the lines '*Hopp, hopp, hopp,/ Pferdchen lauf galopp*' ('Hop, hop, hop,/ Little horse gallop', *BB* 25), sung by his father, or at school when the children roar, '*O Tannenbaum, O Tannenbaum/ Wie grün sind deine Blätter!*' ('O Christmas Tree, O Christmas Tree/ Your branches green delight us', *BB* 35). In these two moments, we see the bonds between Baumgartner and his father, and Baumgartner and his peer group; the use of German points directly towards the cultural roots of his origins and sociality. More often, the lines of German song or nursery rhyme do not arise directly from the context but comment obliquely on it. They seem almost intrusive and can be found at specific moments when the narrative records the disruptions of Baumgartner's bond with his parents or with his peers. In this respect, they plot the trajectory of Baumgartner's displacement, one that begins in early childhood even as he struggles to identify himself and his place within the German bourgeois milieu.

The nursery rhymes speak of a fantasy landscape and characters similar to those found in fairy-tales. As Desai indicates in 'A Secret Connivance', legends, in the forms of fairy-tales, capture a child's imagination and help shape it along orthodox lines.[5] The German songs in *Baumgartner's Bombay* foreground the subliminal process of Hugo's early acculturation; among them, the song of the rider, which recurs in various forms, articulates the processes of Hugo's identity formation and displacement. Lines from the song, first sung to him by his father in a playful moment of paternal male bonding, reappear in a variant form on a later occasion, immediately following an account of childhood disappointment. Hugo wants desperately to be taken to the races, a leisure activity that in his home and, by implication, the bourgeois culture beyond, is adult and exclusively male. Frustrated in his desire as his father leaves alone, Hugo is left with his mother:

> The door slammed. Then Hugo moved, with a roar. He ran to the window and beat on the glass as if to break it, so that his mother had to hold him away even if she was kicked and beaten.
>
> 'Hugo,' she said at last... 'Hugo, I have never been either.'
>
> He looked at her with the hatred of one prisoner for another.
>
> > '*Hoppe, hoppe, Reiter,*
> > *Wenn er fällt, dann schreit er.*
> > *Fällt er in die Hecken,*
> > *fressen ihn die Schnecken,*
> > *fällt er in den Klee,*
> > *schreit er gleich: O weh...*'
> >
> > ['Hop, hop, the rider,
> > When he falls he yells out,
> > If he falls into the hedges
> > The snails eat him up
> > If he falls into the clover
> > He cries out at once: "woe is me"...'][6]

(*BB* 34–5)

The verse, with its motif of riding, appears as a parodic gloss on the melodrama of the child's rejection by the father and his resentment, in turn, of being tied to his mother in a bond of subjection. More significantly, it comments on young Hugo's inability to assume and act out a role of his own choice and refers this disablement to archetypal situations (encoded in the song itself) of frustration, impotence, and loss of self-identity. He is both the prisoner, marginalized from society, and a singular instance of a cultural archetype of failure, the fallen rider. The child Hugo's alienation is entered into German culture, while the narrative re-enacts culture as the incidental and quotidian experience of one of its subjects.

Like the song of the rider, some of the other nursery rhymes also insinuate the dark side of childhood experience: the frustration of desire which dislodges any secure perceptions of self-identity or social place. In another telling episode, the young Hugo experiences the sensation of being out of place in his own school room. He cannot bring himself to claim the Christmas gift proffered by his teacher, and as a result, the gift, which he had so desired, goes to another child, Elizabeth Klein. Interrupting the narrative of shame and embarrassment, focalized by Hugo's perspective, is another extract from a German nursery rhyme:

> 'Schlaf, Kindlein, schlaf!
> Da draussen gehn zwei Schaf!
> Ein schwarzes und ein weisses,
> und wenn das Kind nicht schlafen will,
> dann kommt das Schwarz und beisst es
> Schlaf, Kindlein, Schlaf!'

> ['Sleep, little child, sleep!
> Outside there are two sheep going by!
> A black one and a white one
> And if the child doesn't want to go to sleep
> The black one will come and bite it
> Sleep, little child, sleep!']

(BB, 37)

In the rhyme, which captures a nightmarish, punitive world, the contrast between inside and outside, white sheep and black sheep, maps the cultural polarities of integration and dislocation onto the ethical division of good and evil. It casts the non-conformist – the child who refuses to sleep – as outsider, prey to negative forces.

One might read racist undertones in the verse, and it is tempting to do so because Baumgartner is a Jew in Germany. But in the narrative of childhood, Desai resists overt reconstructions of the modern history of Germans and Jews as persecutor–victim. Elizabeth Klein, who as teacher's favourite benefited from Baumgartner's loss, has an ethnically indeterminate surname. Furthermore, the absence of Hebraic texts or a Jewish discourse throughout the narrative of childhood reaffirms by contrast the singular determinacy of German. Baumgartner is equally ill at ease when he transfers to a school for Jewish children, and, in a further twist of irony, it is in the Jewish school that he is first stigmatized, in Germany, for his Jewishness: '*Baumgartner, Baum, hat ein Nase wie ein Daum!* Baumgartner's dumb, has a nose like a thumb!' (*BB* 38) It is also in the Jewish school that he has a first glimpse of the alienation and displacement that will constitute his identity:

One morning in the school had taught him the tactics for surviving,

'*Hänschen klein, geht allein,*
in die weite Welt hinein,
Stock und Hut stehn ihm gut,
ist ganz wohlgemut.
Doch die Mutter weinet sehr,
hat ja nun kein Hänschen mehr...'

['Little Hans, walking alone
Out into the wide world alone
His stick and hat suit him well
Is in a cheerful mood
But his mother is crying bitterly
She has no little Hans any more'...]

(*BB* 38)

The song is again German, its protagonist the indisputably Germanic '*Hänschen*', and it offers the outsider a cultural model of self-identity as exile from home and place of origin. Baumgartner's later journey to India rehearses the classic colonialist pattern of the dispossessed displaced from the metropolis to the margins. The pattern is set in motion by the increasing intensity of Nazi persecution which leads to the suicide of Hugo's father and the dispossession of mother and son. But the narrative of childhood is not simply another fictional reimagination of the Jewish diaspora. The roots of Baumgartner's colonial exile reach deep into his process of identity formation – in other words, into German bourgeois culture which at once alienates him and offers him a model for his alienation. The forlorn maternal figure in the song speaks to his broken connection with the Germany he leaves behind. In his last backward look before he goes into life-long exile, Baumgartner sees his mother 'standing with her hand on the chest of drawers with yellow cut-glass handles on which she had placed her volumes of Goethe, framed by two puce curtains and a pattern of steam-pipes painted to look like bronze' (*BB*, 57). His entire German self is reduced to this retrospective glance, from the outside, on a tableau-like scene. He is literally and symbolically outside the frame; his German past, symbolized in the figure of his mother, is imprisoned in the frame as she appears frozen in the tableau. And the frame, as sign of the re-presentation of his past, moves between the everyday ordinariness of the 'puce curtains' and the fantasy of the *trompe l'oeil* 'steam-pipes'. In his later memory, his mother and, by implication, his German past, take on the surreal quality of the tableau which he cannot access.

In exile, Baumgartner's deculturation takes corporeal and linguistic form. Arriving in Venice, where he waits for the boat to take him to India, he wanders round the city whose maritime geography and historical situation between east and west, metropolis and margin, emblematizes his own transition. At this point in the narrative, the song of the rider, criss-crossing his childhood reappears.

'*Hopp, hopp, hopp!*
Pferdchen lauf galopp!
Über Stock und über Steine,
aber brich dir nicht die Beine!
Hopp, hopp, hopp!
Pferdchen lauf galopp!'

'Hop, hop, hop!
Little horse gallop!
Up hill and down dale
But mind you don't break your legs!
Hop hop hop
Little horse gallop!'

(*BB* 57)

The sense of liberation – tempered by caution – in the song is counteracted by the anxiety which besets Baumgartner in Venice. Instead of the hearty *'galopp'* that the song urges, his movement in Venice is an aimless perambulation between ethnic retrieval and projections of a new culturally indeterminate self. At one point, alone and nervous, he spots a woman reading a Hebrew newspaper in a café and feels the urge to make contact with her. This momentary recognition of a linguistic bond seems to open up the possibility of 'a new identity, one that suited him, one that he enjoyed' (*BB* 62). But the desire to be relocated to his own ethnic community is soon overtaken by an alternative perception of a culturally indeterminate self-identity:

> Venice *was* the East, and yet it was Europe too; it was that magic boundary where the two met and blended, and for those seven days Hugo had been part of their union. He realised it only now: that during his ... ceaseless walking, he had been drawing closer and closer to this discovery of that bewitched point where they became one land of which he felt himself the natural citizen.
>
> It made him forget the Jewish woman ... (*BB* 63)

A crisis of identity is temporarily reconstructed as a rediscovery of self. History – his own and as the collective experience of diaspora – has cast Baumgartner as outsider, a marginal, but marginality is here reconstrued as release from a self that is spatially, and hence culturally and historically, defined, and as relocation at that 'bewitched point', that 'land', or space, of a new hybrid self that straddles east and west and belongs to neither. History has not redirected Baumgartner towards an identity reconstituted in ethnic and racial terms. Instead, it has worked in more insidious ways by seeming to proffer the chance of disrupting those cultural prescriptions encoded in the German nursery rhymes and fairy-tales and to map the 'magic boundary' of his own self. The shifting linguistic markers in the narrative of Baumgartner's life after his arrival in India show how Venice holds out a promise of emancipation which, in the decree of fate, will not be for someone like him.

On his first arrival in India, Baumgartner

> found he had to build a new language to suit these new conditions – German no longer sufficed, and English was elusive. Languages

sprouted around him like topical foliage and he picked words from it without knowing if they were English or Hindi or Bengali – they were simply words he needed: *chai, khana, baraf, lao, jaldi, jota, chota peg, pani, kamra, soda, garee...* what was this language he was wrestling out of the air, wrenching around to his own purposes? He suspected it was not Indian, but India's, the India he was marking out for himself. (*BB* 92)

Once unfixed from its German origins, Baumgartner's linguistic identity has become purely contingent, and in the free creativity which enables him to remake himself and mark out his own space, he experiences a utopian moment of liberation. But in professing no allegiance to any particular system of significa-tion, the self is cut off from the perceptions of reality that are encoded in and enclosed by the different systems and help stabilize its relations with the outside world. That 'bewitched point' on which Baumgartner has thought to relocate himself dissolves, at moments, into the vantage point of the surreal. As he recalls the plethora of sight and sound that is India, the corporeal world, he 'wondered if it had not all been a mirage, a dream' (*BB* 93). He is poised on the confrontation between his own 'magic boundary' and India as physical place that is the domain of time and history.

This confrontation never takes place because of Baumgart-ner's stuttering tactics of survival. His linguistic incapacities, the source of his contingent self, consign him to the outskirts of the discourse of the expatriate communities and his Indian contacts. In the narrative, India remains ineluctably alien, from the moment of Baumgartner's first arrival, when he looks in vain for 'a signboard ... in a familiar language' (*BB* 53), to the last days of his life, after fifty years, when he feels 'uncertain as ever of which language to employ' (*BB* 6) to greet a native watchman. Unplaced in any of India's linguistic communities, he is detached from the vicissitudes of personal relationships or their fluctuations in the historical tide that sweeps India from colonialism to war and independence. In its alterity, India is kept at bay; for a long time, it shows little interest in either penetrating or disallowing Baumgartner's 'India'. Reticent among the riches of the languages that surround him, Baumgartner has renegotiated his alienation from Europe as the condition of his survival as an alien in India. The title of the novel, *Baumgartner's Bombay*, mimics those of the Baedeker's guides to European cities, which ostensibly open up an alien space to the interested tourist, but in doing so also reduce this space to comprehensible form and enable the tourist to possess it as his own. *Baumgartner's Bombay* shows the transformation of an Indian location to a space made in the protagonist's image, an interior landscape constituted of fragments appropriated from the external world.

Significantly, in the internment camp for enemy aliens, where it seems both Europe and India have closed in on him, Baumgartner's mode of self-definition is silence. The camp replicates the historical divisions that brought it into being: Nazi sympathizers, tolerated by a demoralized British colonial authority, covertly attack Jewish aliens. As German, as Jew, as colonialist, Baumgartner straddles these divisions, but is para-doxically also an outsider to all of them; he could neither enter into nor refuse the discourses of each. While the inmates share anxieties about the war and their condition, Baumgartner remains silent: 'he shed nothing...like a mournful turtle – he carried everything with him... [S]ilence was his natural condi-tion' (*BB* 109, 117). Vestiges of his German past reappear, but they are increasingly worked upon by memory to become the building blocks of a self-identity perceived in a new set of relations with the world. The process takes shape during one of those prolonged periods of inertia and silence when he noticed a woman prisoner hanging up her washing, and longs for the domestic routine that she enacts which is 'simple, routine, repetitive, calm'. In her, he misrecognizes – or reinvents – his German childhood: 'He had not known women like her in Germany... and yet she seemed to embody his German child-hood – at least, *he chose to see her as such an embodiment, it was pleasant to do so, like humming a children's song*' (*BB* 126–7, emphasis added).

The German past is transformed, and becomes a 'children's song' that, unlike the songs we have seen, is transported in time away from its culture-specific functions. Germany is resignified as the realm of nostalgia, the repository of the lost innocence of simpler times. This idyll, so apparently a construct of memory, also projects a self-identity released from the chaos of language and languages; the song is hummed, that is, voiced without words. In a further step from his earlier contingent self, Baumgartner aspires towards the idyll of silence where the work ritual requires minimal verbal exchange. This mnemonic remaking of Germany is mapped onto an earlier moment of the narrative when Baumgartner watches some Indian women working in the fields outside the camp. From 'his initial bewilderment at lives so primitive, so basic and unchanging, he began to envy them that simplicity, the absence of choice and history. By comparison, his own life seemed hopelessly tangled and unsightly, symbolised aptly by the strands of barbed wire wrapped around the wooden posts and travelling in circles and double circles around the camp' (*BB* 110–11). These two moments speak to each other in a dialogue that relocates the transformed German past in the Indian present. They define the 'magic boundary' as a space not only abstracted from east and west but also unbound by time and history in which the subject has no agency, nor need of it. In the women he sees, the maternal bond, which in the German song discussed earlier signifies Baumgartner's connection with his cultural origins, is refigured and transposed as the cornerstone of the magical, timeless world.

In the camp, the only communication that Baumgartner actively longs for is from his mother whom he left behind in Germany. The tragic impracticability of the magical in the real is captured in the languages of her postcards which he finally obtains after his release and which he carefully preserves throughout his life in India. In another context, Judie Newman has argued that the 'meaninglessness, perpetual recurrence and blankness' which are the impressions created by the postcards from Baumgartner's mother point towards the historical reality of the German concentration camps which is replicated in the internment camp in India.[7] Each of these postcards

> bore a stamped message that read, '*Rückantwort nur an Postkarten in deutscher Sprache.*' What officialdom had they passed through, giving them this chilling aspect? 'Answers on postcards only, in German.' Only the endearments were familiar: '*Meine kleine Maus*', '*Mein Häschen*', and the signature: 'Mutti', 'Muttilein', 'Mü'. Apart from them, the messages were strangely empty, repetitive and cryptic. 'Keep well, my rabbit. Do not worry. I am well. Where are you, my mouse? Are you well? I am well. Do not worry. I have enough. Have

you enough? Mutti. Mu.' Nothing more.
There was none dated later than February 1941. (*BB* 164)

The language of the maternal bond is circumscribed and estranged by an official language, imperious and imperative, whose authorizing discourse Baumgartner fears but cannot understand. The familiar language of his past is completely undermined in the historical process that has produced a different German language, a different German reality. History, in a mockery of his aspiration, intrudes to empty his own past of meaning and produces a past whose meaning he cannot grasp, but this is a message which he does not, or cannot, read.

Returning to the postcards again and again in India, he tries to extrapolate from their languages some coherent meaning from the past that could direct him towards the magical space of his aspiration. At the end of the day, when his alienation from India is complete, he appropriates those maternal endearments, the linguistic remnants of a former identity, to sustain his life. In the flat that he shares with his cats, he talks to them in vestiges of the maternal language: 'Fritzi, *du alte* Fritzi, *komm*, Fritzi,' and 'Ach, *Liebchen*, Lise, Lise' (*BB* 146). His uneasy socializing with the café owner – his single point of contact with the Indian world – is directed by the need to obtain food for the cats. Of the other people he has met since arriving in India, only Lotte, the drunken German showgirl, remains. In her, the maternal figure from his past, displaced onto the women he sees in the camp, undergoes its decadent refiguring in the real world. In a twist of irony – the most savage in Desai's fiction so far – the 'magic boundary' Baumgartner aspires to materialize as his almost complete alienation from India as place and its history of decolonization and independence. Shrinking into his own world, he feels 'his life blur, turn grey, like a curtain wrapping him in its dusty felt' (*BB* 211); this self-imposed cocoon resonates as much of death as of protected survival. If Baumgartner, like many of Desai's protagonists, comes to realize that he has 'never been a part of the mainstream' (*BB* 211), this realization of difference is neither the sign of valour nor the turn towards a comic resolution, but the sign of how his survival has been an oversight of fate whose full capriciousness is inscribed in his history.

Working through another legacy of history – the one signified by the oppressive public language of the postcard – which Baumgartner has managed to elude, fate now suddenly ensnares him, and with a vengeance. It appears in the person of the blond, drug-crazed German youth whose refusal to leave the café Baumgartner frequents threatens his own welcome there. To Farrokh, the café owner, they were both 'just *firanghi*' (*BB* 21) who have no place in his domain, and he puts pressure on Baumgartner to talk to the young man in German. In order to secure the source of food for his cats, Baumgartner reluctantly yields to the pressure, and manages to remove the young addict to his flat. In the flat, the addict admits, ' "I am *krank – furchtbar krank*," he broke into German.' His first words were 'like a crack in a poorly built dyke and now the flood poured out, streaming over Baumgartner and the cats and the dinner and the whole of the shabby dark room, filling it and setting it afloat on visions of places and people that had never entered before, even in nightmares' (*BB* 156). In direct contrast to the German endearments, the 'mother-tongue', the German the young addict speaks, as he narrates his adventures in India, performs the discourse of bloodshed, slaughter, and death. Desai does not crudely represent the German addict as the direct successor to the Nazi past, although the novel does emphasize his Aryan, as opposed to Baumgartner's Jewish, lineage. He appears as the symbolic detritus of the historical tide that moulded and remoulded German culture before and after the war. He is a wanderer, another marginal like Baumgartner, but also one from the opposite end of the German racial and cultural spectrum. So, too, is his sickness. While the disability of Baumgartner's upbringing makes India intimidating and alien, the young man's diseased mind constructs an orientalist nightmare out of an Indian landscape and ethnic rituals and customs. In their confrontation, the young German and Baumgartner enact the tragic meaning of the message of the postcards, a message decreed by history. Unhinged by drugs, the young man returns one evening and stabs Baumgartner repeatedly as he sleeps. A German, and by implication, European struggle, which has engulfed the colonial margins, reaches its final conclusion in a postcolonial setting that has seceded from it and to which it is merely the struggle of the '*firanghi*'.

As he lies in bed during the last moments before the young man returns, Baumgartner rereads the packet of postcards:

> Gradually the words ran into each other, became garbled. They made no sense. Nothing made sense. Germany there, India here – India there, Germany here. Impossible to capture, to hold, to read them, make sense of them. They all fell away from him, into an abyss... He stood watching as they fell and floated, floated and fell, till they drifted out of sight, silently, and he was left on the edge, clutching his pyjamas, straining to look. But there was nothing to look at, it was all gone, and he shut his eyes, to receive the darkness that flooded in, poured in and filled the vacuum with the thick black ink of oblivion, of *Nacht und Nebel*. (*BB* 215–16)

The nightmarish world of the childhood song, '*Schlaf, Kindlein, schlaf!*' is, in retrospect, prophetic; its menacing warning of death to the conscious outsider is here realized. Baumgartner, who has struggled to stay awake, to make sense out of being an outsider, apprehends the senselessness of his struggle in this moment filled with the tragic pathos and determinism. In sleep, in the surrender of consciousness, he fulfils his cultural and historical destiny laid down in the message of the song. This sleep is the dissolution of boundaries that will finally deplete him of all self. It will also lift him out of time: the 'magic boundary' in its final transformation into the 'abyss' of non-being. In the last cruel twist of irony, Baumgartner's dim awareness of the 'abyss' is encoded in his native German: '*Nacht und Nebel*'.

In *Clear Light of Day* and *In Custody*, Desai has created Indian characters who have come to terms with the past in ways that enable agency and a dignified survival in the present. The radical differences between pre- and post-independence India are inscribed in the difficult struggles and adjustments that Bim and Deven feel compelled to make. In stepping outside India, *Baumgartner's Bombay* points the struggle with history and fate towards a European culture whose racist and colonialist past not only dislocates its own subjects but also leaves a legacy of alienation, mutual indifference and hostility between west and east that continues to endure. For those caught in this history, like Baumgartner and his coinhabitants of the novel, the gestures of survival are painful, undignified, and in the end recoil upon themselves.

From a postcolonial vantage, Baumgartner's memory and retrieval of his 'mother-tongue' can be seen as a desperate attempt to 'reappropriate the language of one's expropriation, to reclaim the German from its Nazi past'.[8] In his memory of German as the language of childhood and maternal love, Baumgartner uses the very signs of Nazi persecution – stamped indelibly on the postcards – to make meaning of where he comes from and hence, what he is. This act of self-making, which is also an act of resistance sustains him in his long years as exile in India, and, in the context of Desai's fiction, creates a solidarity between him and other characters – Nanda, Bim, Deven – whose prosaic, everyday existence is a constant struggle to reconceive the past in order to set themselves free. Deven's poetry is Baumgartner's song, an art of expression derived from others in the past and transformed into themselves. That Baumgartner's resistance in German is overwhelmed by the reincarnation, in the blond youth, of German as the language of the persecutor is the devastating irony – and ultimate tragedy – of Desai's novel. The young man's phantasmagoric narrative estranges India so that it recalls the horror and nightmare of the unutterably alien that is the landscape of the Holocaust. As the sign of selfhood and the nemesis of the self, German speaks of Baumgartner as his own alterity, the subject as the inhabitation of familiarity and strangeness, what is at home, and the unhomely. Bombay is Indian and Baumgartner's place of abode; it is also Baumgartner's Bombay, German and ineluctably foreign.

4

Firanghi

'*Firanghi*': to Farroukh, the café owner whom Baumgartner sees everyday, this is who Baumgartner is and always will be, no matter how long he has lived in India. Like its synonyms in other Asian languages – 'gaijin' in Japanese and 'gwai lo' in Cantonese spring to mind – '*firanghi*' resonates of more than just its semantic translation as 'foreigner'. Implicated in the word is a derogatory verbal gesture at a subject-formation who is outside the indigenous social pale, and a naming of that anxiety felt by the indigene at the stranger's presence in his community. The stranger, according to Zygmunt Bauman, is neither friend nor enemy, and unincorporable into the binary opposition of the two. He can shift between the two sides or terms of the opposition, and because he is constituted in the in-between, his presence threatens 'the sociation itself – the very *possibility* of sociation'.[1] If estrangement and homelessness as conditions of existence are recurrent concerns in Desai's fiction, they certainly haunt her narratives about foreigners in India. Before Baumgartner, the foreigner-as-stranger is the subject of the short story 'Scholar and Gypsy', published in *Games at Twilight,* about two Americans in India. More recently, in *Journey to Ithaca* (1995), Desai once again coordinates her interests in the foreigner in India and India in world history which we have seen in *Baumgartner's Bombay,* to set in motion a new fictional dialogue about home and homelessness, home and the world. In these works, the *firanghi* – the foreigner-as-stranger who is at once friend and foe, embarked on a journey in India which can only be a foreign quest, at home in India and inevitably homeless – is that problematic subject whose presence forces India to turn inside out, to estrange from itself, in order to recognize and negotiate his or her difference. Desai's fiction about foreigners in

India participates actively in India's self-estrangement, and its cross-cultural recognition and negotiation of difference.

In its title, 'Scholar and Gypsy' sets up clearly the opposite positions of the American couple David and Pat, and their arrival and passage through India are marked by their experience of this opposition on a number of levels. David is a dull character, a sociology student identified by a view of 'India' as object of inquiry, who cannot begin to understand why 'India' seems to overwhelm his wife. Pat's distress is evident from the very first sentence of the story – 'Her first day in Bombay wilted her.' (*GT* 108) – and the narrative recurrently embodies in her physical torments a progressive inner disintegration. The various postures of Pat's body speak of dislocation: 'If she stepped out of the air-conditioned hotel room, she drooped, her head hung, her eyes glazed, she felt faint' (*GT* 108). But, above all, it is what she sees which continuously unsettles her: 'the bar in the hotel was so crowded, the people there were so large and vital and forceful in their brilliant clothes and with their metallic voices and their eyes that flashed over her like barber's shears, cutting and exposing, that she felt crushed rather than revived' (*GT* 109). This is a strange and disturbing first encounter with "India", and it sets the tone for most of Pat's early experience. The experience is always tactile, as it is here, composed of bodies in press and motion whose impact upon Pat herself is, in turn, expressed through her body and particularly its discomposition. In the biological and cultural ecology of Bombay, Pat struggles to survive as an alien. If to the indigene the foreigner is a source of anxiety, 'India', to Pat as foreigner, is an aggressive physical presence threatening violence to the self.

Through the eyes of Pat, "India" becomes animated in a way which David never sees. Besides motion, it develops colour and substance, but it continues to resist either form or definition. In the party hosted by a rich Bombay businessman, Pat observes that

> The guests all wore brilliant clothes and jewellery, and their eyes and teeth flashed with such primitive lust as they eyed her slim, white-sheathed blonde self, that the sensation of being caught up and crushed, crowded in and choked sent her into corners where their knees pushed into her, their hands slid over her back, their voices bored into her, so that when she got back to the hotel, on

David's arm, she was more like a corpse than an American globe-
trotter. (*GT* 109)

From Pat's point of view, the menace of urban and bourgeois
'India' is palpable; the excess of colour and glitter intrudes upon
her, like a kind of alien possession sapping her of vigour and
life. The perceived sense of the 'primitive' is also recurrent –
'primitive' is the word which the increasingly distraught Pat
invokes to describe the people she encounters, and their
appearance and behaviour. It is a word borrowed from David's
ethnographic lexicon but which she, in her distress, glosses with
an explanation entirely her own, and it becomes the convenient
label – not unlike '*firanghi*' – for the predatorial strangeness of
the social environment. Associated with this word are images
that re-present human beings as bestial or grossly material: Mr
Gidwani, the rich host of the party, has a 'face like an amiable
baboon' and his wife, 'a chocolate pudding belly' (*GT* 111).

Driven out of Bombay by her distress, the couple arrives in
Delhi. In the unfolding environmental and cultural diversity of
India, Bombay, as a kind of jungle, is replaced by Delhi as desert,
dry and dusty, which to Pat is equally inhospitable and life-
threatening. In Delhi, the threat rises not so much from the
press and swell of human bodies, and the sheer pressure of
material surfeit, but seems to emanate from the signs of
traditional heritage and culture. Following David's advice to
amuse herself with Indian art, she visits the antique shops of
Delhi, only to rush out after less than an hour,

> horror rising in her throat like vomit. She felt pursued by the
> primitive, the elemental and barbaric ... recalling those great heavy
> bosoms of bronze and stone, the hips rounded and full as water-
> pots, the flirtatious little bells on ankles and bellies, the long, sly eyes
> that curved out of the voluptuous stone faces, not unlike those of the
> shopkeepers themselves with their sibilant, inviting voices. (*GT* 113)

A visit to a social worker in Delhi and the crèche she runs does
not offer Pat the relief of another vantage, for while she observes
meticulously the children eating and writing, she remains
distant from the aspect of 'India' they reveal.

It is tempting to label and dismiss Pat as colonialist and
orientalist, but to do so would occlude Desai's acute perception
of the ethnic and cultural disorientation experienced by the

young western – and white – woman on her first visit to India. Beyond prejudicial labelling, what we are invited to see in Pat's response is sheer incomprehension and her struggle for cognition by reframing alterity in comprehensible terms. Pat is not unlike the child wrenched from familiar surroundings, and displaced into a space which is frightening, close, and closing in. Her language of cognition – to know the unknown – is derived from David, who has the authority of formal knowledge, but it is resignified within a childish and childlike scheme of things – flashing lights, bright colours, hissing noises, jungle animals, chocolate pudding, statues that come to life. Pat is an adult thrust back by her encounters with 'India' into a child's world of sensation and fantastical metamorphosis, except that the world re-appears, or returns, as nightmare rather than as pleasurable fairy-tale. In the short story, as we shall see, Desai shows how both Pat and David are subjects of their own histories; their past, which they carry within them, frames their present recognition or misrecognition of 'India'. 'India', for them, is the site of catalysis where their American past is activated in the present in the fulfilment of their identities. It is in this way that Desai represents them as truly *firanghi*: India is a place of transition where they act out their ineluctably foreign past.

It is interesting to consider whether Desai considers Pat and David's experience as specifically American or generally typical of foreigners in India. The protagonists of 'Scholar and Gypsy', *Baumgartner's Bombay*, and *Journey to Ithaca* are of different national and cultural provenance although, like most of Desai's Indian protagonists, they too come from middle-class back-grounds. There is also a shared perception among most of them of India as exotic or the site of mystical experiences, and, consciously or unconsciously, of their journey as a quest. But if Desai is interested in her fiction to represent the variety and fine discriminations among her middle-class Indian characters, she is equally perceptive about how her foreign characters embody the differences of their own cultural locations. We have seen how the young Aryan in *Baumgartner's Bombay* enacts the return of a German past from which Baumgartner is dislocated or thinks he has escaped, in order not only to expose the actuality that he remains foreign in the eyes of people among whom he has lived for most of his life, but also to drive him to his ultimate and unutterable alienation in death itself. There is, for Baumgartner, no escaping the past. From a similar vantage but with a different focus, Pat and David's American past catches up with them in India to determine their arrival, passage, and separate destinations. As we shall see later on in this chapter, Sophie and Matteo, the Italian couple in *Journey to Ithaca*, represent a complicated rewriting of the story of Pat and David after Desai's own venture out of the Indian milieu into world history in *Baumgartner's Bombay*. Her desire to explore other histories in their different engagements with India can be seen in her allocation of different cultural origins to her foreign characters. The popular western perception of India as an exotic and mystical destination is actualized and critiqued, but always with sympathy and understanding of the trials and tribulations which travelling in India entails for foreigners in search of enlightenment, and the pleasures and disappointments which attend their quest. In her fiction, Desai recognizes the indigenous stigmatizing of '*firanghi*', but also implements complicated acts of re-signification which relocate the sign on the permeable borders of inside and outside, home and homelessness, India and the world.

To return, for the time being, to 'Scholar and Gypsy'. If Pat's initial response to India is incomprehension, fear, and at best, a sense of unbridgeable distance, then David is equally mystified by his wife's seeming inability to see through his own lens of observation. The third-person narrative of Pat and revelations of her interiority are often contrasted with David's vantage on her, and it is through this contrast that Pat's multi-dimensionality as fictional subject emerges. As this happens, David becomes increasingly identified by his frustration with Pat, which, in turn, reveals his shortcomings as anthropologist and husband. The story is, in this respect, about the failure of their marriage brought on by their irreconcilable experiences of India. David is shocked by Pat's notions of the primitive; to him, urban India is not primitive enough and this points to his scholarly identification of native culture with the traditional and the underdeveloped, an identification not uncommon among anthropologists of his generation trained in the discipline in Anglo-American academies.[2]

Implicitly challenged by Pat, he seeks to reassert his authority, and the struggle between his cognition of India and hers is the pronounced theme of the second half of the story; this begins with Pat and David's departure from the city for the country, as Desai takes her readers to another, and radically different, geography and cultural ecology, which is also India. In the mountains around the small country town of Manali, Pat recovers her equanimity of spirit and spontaneity of character; she is able to map this Indian landscape onto her own childhood home in a Vermont farm – a childhood which is revealed for the first time in the story. In this remapping, Pat recognizes India as familiar, and quickly begins 'to feel it as home' (*GT* 123). In contrast, David becomes increasingly discomposed, and replicates the alienation from his environment. He refuses to accompany her on her visits to the Tibetan quarter of the town because he cannot face 'the open drain ... the yellow *pai* dogs and abjectly filthy children', and the native artefacts 'presided over by stolid women with faces carved intricately out of hard wood' (*GT* 124). The physical proximity of traditional life ironically defeats him despite his supposed ethnographic preoccupations with the 'primitive', and in an implicit acknowledgement of cognitive failure, he loses interest in the thesis for which he is doing the research. Another expression of his defeat is his denigration of Pat's enthusiasm for the sights and sounds, flora and fauna of Manali, and outrage at her autonomy and agency as she befriends a community of hippies, westerners who have made a home in Manali and become a kind of tourist attraction to Indians on day-trips and holiday visits.

Thus the second half of the story enacts the reversal between Pat and David in their experiences of India. In deciding to join the hippy commune and stay in Manali, Pat goes 'native', so to speak, for the commune is the latest of the incoming ethnic settlements – like that of the Tibetans before – of Manali. As the complications in her situation multiply, the boundaries between 'foreign' and 'native', outside and inside, become increasingly blurred. Going 'native', for Pat, implies a return to her place of nativity in rural Vermont; paradoxically, it also means remaining indelibly foreign, for this is how the hippy community is marked out and perceived by Indians, supposedly natives, who, in another of the story's strategic reversals, appear as tourists

71

and curious outsiders. David, up till now the dominant partner in the marriage, diminishes in both authority and stature until he becomes a figure of farce who, in a desperate hurry to leave Manali, is involved in an accident where his face is burnt by steam from the over-heated radiator of a public bus. In the care of the American missionary doctor, he becomes childlike, 'limp and helpless', and as he sips Horlicks and listens to the voice of the doctor 'flow over him like a stream of American milk' (GT 135), he seems to revert to childhood in a mimicry of Pat's experience of 'India' right at the beginning. As the story ends, he arrives back in Delhi, alone and feeling greater regret about 'his face like a painted baboon' (GT 138) from the gentian violet salve over his wounds than about splitting up with his wife. This image of David is superimposed on the image of Mr Gidwani of Bombay who, as we remember, appears to Pat to have 'a face like an amiable baboon'. Through this superimposition, the story seems to suggest that David has become integrated into an 'India' – gone native? – which Pat has earlier recognized or misrecognized. In the final, and remarkable, reversal of the story, David has arrived in the 'India' of his wife's gothic imagination, and his arrival is co-terminous with the start of her relocation in another 'India' of her own making.

There is another strand in the narrative of Pat's transformation which links 'Scholar and Gypsy' with the more recent *Journey to Ithaca*. The disagreement between Pat and David climaxes over her recurrent visits to a temple in the forest around Manali which she thinks is Buddhist but which David, with pompous scholastic rectitude, identifies as Hindu. As he becomes more and more scathing about her ignorance, she becomes increasingly assertive, to the point when, in a final declaration of independence, she screams at him: 'You, you don't even know it's possible to find Buddha in a Hindu temple' (GT 137). In this altercation, Desai connects Pat's physical experience of India with an instinctual aversion to intellectualizing and formal naming. This connection reconstitutes Pat's identity within the frames of her Vermont childhood spent in nature, and enables her to regain composure in her life and find a place in 'India'. Her American beginnings implicitly determine her initial dislocation and her quasi-animistic embrace of the spirit in nature at the end, although in its movement towards a comic-satiric ending, 'Scholar and Gypsy' does not really invest Pat's journey with the significance of a serious mystical quest.

In an interview, Desai has observed:

> I think every writer does tend to use a handful of characters and a handful of themes over and over again. In a way, it is one's obsessions that one walks over and over, and rarely feels one is finished with the subject.[3]

Desai's interest in foreigners may or may not be an 'obsession' but their travels through India in search of enlightenment are certainly a subject she returns to and fleshes out in Matteo in *Journey to Ithaca*, a novel which orchestrates the themes about the foreigner in India outlined in 'Scholar and Gypsy'. And, as in 'Scholar and Gypsy', Matteo's journey is at first shadowed by that of his wife, Sophie, who in the course of the novel emerges into her own story. It is the issue of 'foreignness' which can be seen as an obsession in Desai's fiction, and its recurrence and mutation as structures of questions and answers are complicated by her tragic-comic vantages on home and homelessness, India in world history, and determinism and agency. In the context of the changing problematic of 'foreignness', the foreigner in India is a specific, though not exclusive, embodiment.

The subject of foreigners in India, and their search for mystic illumination has been questioned by two well-known reviewers of *Journey to Ithaca*. J. M. Coetzee sees Matteo and Sophie as uncharacteristic departures from Desai's sympathies for 'the defeated, even the hopelessly defeated', and those 'on the margins of society whose marginality has nothing glamorous or appealingly extreme about it'. To Coetzee, half of *Journey to Ithaca*

> is a mordant chronicle of the vicissitudes of a pair of well-to-do, spoiled European hippies who, on the basis of a reading of Hermann Hesse, travel through India in search of the Supreme Light; the other half is the life of the charismatic old woman, known only as 'The Mother,' in whose ashram the couple end up.[4]

Some of these negative sentiments can already be glimpsed in Meenakshi Mukherjee's earlier review of the Indian edition of the novel. In noting that the edition is published one and a half years after its first appearance in Britain, Mukherjee suggests that 'in all likelihood the novel is not intended for the Indian reader'. She adds,

India is not so much an actual geographical space in this novel as an elusive idea... *Journey to Ithaca* intertwines two such voyages of pilgrims from different parts of the world who seek a mirage called India. Those of us who have to daily confront the concrete dimensions of the Indian reality may not, after all, be so beguiled by its elusive aura.[5]

Both Coetzee and Mukherjee's comments can be located on different but also interlocking points of a postcolonial discourse which critiques Eurocentrism as the historical site of social and economic privilege. Coetzee's 'well-to-do, European hippies' point unambiguously to the subjects of this privilege, and Mukherjee extends, by implication, these subjects to include not only Matteo and Sophie as fictional characters but also those she presumes to be the implied, and foreign, readers of the novel itself. If Coetzee argues broadly in the interest of marginality against the class advantages of Matteo and Sophie, then, to Mukherjee, the location of the margin and those marginalized are in 'Indian reality'. In referring to 'those of us', Mukherjee conjures the spectre of the *firanghi* – the implicit 'them' – but hers is not merely an exclusionary argument, for she is voicing concern about the truth of representation that is displaced by the 'mirage' of 'India' which beguiles those who know nothing about Indian reality with its 'elusive aura'.

Coetzee and Mukherjee's criticisms are oriented by familiar postcolonial contestations about class and arguments from location. While acknowledging the validity of their concerns, it is possible to argue that *Journey to Ithaca* is an effort on Desai's part to rewrite the story of the foreigner in India that, in turn, contests the powerful mediation of texts of European origin over the world's imagination of 'India'. Interestingly, Coetzee has offered a clue to this in his dismissive remark about how Matteo and Sophie embark on their quest 'on the basis of a reading of Hermann Hesse'. Hesse is not only an authority as far as the two protagonists are concerned but also a strong precursor in the German literary tradition which is part of Desai's maternal and linguistic heritage. This is a heritage which she remembers, for the first time, in *Baumgartner's Bombay*, and *Journey to Ithaca* can be seen as a second act in this mnemonic psychodrama.

In some respects, both Coetzee and Mukherjee have missed, or chosen to ignore, the metaphorical configuration of the physical journey through India and the inner passage towards enlightenment which is the burden of Hesse's *Siddhartha* and his writings about India, and which Desai re-embodies in Matteo and Sophie. In his 'Remembrance of India', Hesse has this to say about his Indian journey: 'I not only got to know a strange, exotic land, but in experiencing what was foreign, I found that especially within myself I had discoveries to make and tests to withstand.'[6] *Siddhartha* is a story about India – and a fable of the spiritual quest by a powerful Indian religious and cultural icon – written by a foreigner unperplexed by, if not unconscious of, his European origin and outsider position and the co-optation of cultural difference into European self-identity. In taking up the legacy of Hesse, Desai's story about foreigners *in* India is a revisionist project that is inflected by a late-twentieth-century – and post-Orientalist – sense of knowingness and irony about questions of representation and who speaks, and who has the right to speak, for whom. In *Journey to Ithaca*, Desai transforms Hesse's 'Indian' fable into a contemporary novel which may not be about India as it is daily known to its inhabitants, but is nonetheless realistic in the sense that Hesse's own mystical quest, displaced onto Siddhartha, is now returned to where it is embodied in reality; that is, in the character of the foreigner himself. Furthermore, in the light of the exclusionary label, *firanghi*, by which even a long-time resident of India like Baumgartner is stigmatized, Desai, in *Journey to Ithaca*, re-identifies the foreigner as marginal not only in Matteo and Sophie but also through the figure of the 'Mother' who is of Egyptian-French origin. This re-identification gives the lie to Coetzee's disparagement of the novel as being centred on spoiled Europeans, and his related assumption that Desai has turned her back on marginality.

To begin with Matteo and Sophie.[7] Matteo is a voluntary exile from Europe, seeking in 'India' a refuge from the inhibiting bourgeois home of his Italian 'Mama', only to find it in the ashram of the woman guru, the 'Mother'. In its ironical revisits to the 'mother'-place, Matteo's life-journey exemplifies the negotiation between determinism and agency earlier sketched in Pat. Matteo's childhood and early life in Italy, narrated in the Prologue, is noticeable for the sense of entrapment he feels within his provincial bourgeois family. In this narrative of beginnings, extended beyond that of 'Scholar and Gypsy', Desai gives the foreigner in India a history before arrival in order to reaffirm what she has already shown in *Baumgartner's Bombay* – that his dislocation begins not in India but, literally and metaphorically, at home, in his own family and natal place. From these beginnings, Matteo's journey in India takes shape as a doubled quest for refuge not only from a stifling bourgeois past but for an inner self no longer out of its element that is the true significance of homeliness.

Like Baumgartner, Matteo has a stern father and doting mother; bourgeois culture, inscribed in his immediate and extended family of uncles and cousins, is represented as individualistic, self-obsessed, and above all masculine, and Matteo is clearly a misfit – similar to Raka in *Fire on the Mountain* – the child whose frustrations and intense emotional personality can find no expression in the human society in which fate has placed him. To counteract the artificiality of his parental home, Matteo seeks respite in nature, preferring to spend long periods in the surrounding countryside, first alone, and later in the company of his English tutor, Fabian. It was Fabian who introduced him to the writings of Hesse and Blake, and through the references to these writings, Desai shows how the metaphors and rhetoric of Romanticism become one of the languages of identity shaping Matteo's incipient self-recognition and cognition of his place in the world. Unlike the individualistic and material obsessions of bourgeois culture, Matteo manifests an early interest in the intersubjective relations between man and nature; being 'natural' is, in the course of the novel, mapped onto the quest for spiritual enlightenment. The space of Matteo's quest, as his reading of Hesse and Fabian's tutelage orient him, is India.

Sophie attracted Matteo because at their first meeting, she appeared 'totally unaffected by the surroundings and the company' (*JI* 30) of his bourgeois home setting. This is an early indication of her difference from him who is so completely ill at ease, but the fact that his mother disapproves of her informal manner and dress also identifies her as a kindred spirit. The ambivalence of difference and identification haunts them throughout their journey in India; in this, and in Sophie's experience on arrival, the novel rewrites and expands the story of 'Scholar and Gypsy'. Like Pat's, Sophie's arrival in India is marked by a strong sense of unease and discomfort as she follows Matteo in his search which takes them into cheap hotel rooms, the gloomy interiors of houses and ashrams, and other enclosed spaces. Contrary to her expectations of exotic sights and sounds, 'India', for Sophie, has moved resolutely indoors, – as it did for Pat – present not only in the shades of poverty and decay, but also lodging itself in her, disorienting her self-identity so that she becomes increasingly frustrated, irritable, and uncomprehending of what and where she is, and why she is there. In this discomposition of interiority, Sophie's apparent subordination to Matteo becomes visible in another form as her intense love for him, and this love is an individuating experience as much as it unsettles her and conflicts with her unique desires and difference from him. The narrative opposes the two faces of the woman's experience of love, but also moves to articulate them: Sophie tries out different communities as Matteo searches for his ideal ashram; he is sullen and resentful wherever he tries to settle down, but she always goes back to him, and follows him on his journeys through India. His journey is her journey; her journey, as we shall see, takes her to realms of experience which map onto his but also develop its full sense of difference.

In narrating their travels, *Journey to Ithaca* unfolds a rich tapestry of the geography and ecological diversities of India; as in most of Desai's novels, descriptions of the natural environment, interacting with social scenes and manners that are acutely observed, actualize India as physical location. At the same time, the optic on language and cultural identity in *Baumgartner's Bombay* is renewed in that Matteo and Sophie's experiences of 'India' can be seen in terms of their contact with the different discourses which mediate the foreigner's knowledge of place. In the first chapter, which narrates the period of their arrival, their companions are mostly travellers and expatriates of western origin, others like them who seek alternative ways of living and experiences. These communities – or perhaps groups would be a more appropriate description since their transient members do not enjoy close or enduring bonds of affiliation – wander from one place to another, drawn by stories they hear that are retold from traveller to traveller, of arcane and exotic experiences and availability of cheap drugs. It is these often lurid tales circulating among the itinerant members of the group to which Sophie and Matteo first attach themselves that frame their early knowledge of India as a physical location, and lay down the itinerary – or plot – of their own travels.

But already in these days of first arrival, there is a conflict between verbal narrative and the non-verbal in Matteo's strenuous quest for spiritual illumination. In attempting to break free of tales which press him and Sophie back among the physically degenerate crowd of hippies and foreign vagrants, he spends longer and longer periods on his own, silent and among silence. In a passage which recalls the short story 'Surface Textures', the text shows Matteo staring and staring at a stone lodged in a tree trunk, until 'he saw that what was perfectly balanced there in a cleft in the tree was not a stone at all but a circle, and it contained within it another circle, and another; that there was no beginning and no end to them; they were infinite; they were infinity' (*JI* 68). These episodes of isolation become increasingly frequent until Matteo collapses from nervous exhaustion; he is drawn back into the world of language when the Indian doctor Sophie takes him to admonishes him, and counsels reading and study, rather than the hope of revelation, as the path to spiritual illumination. But in the first ashram where he stays in order to pursue his studies, the world continues to manifest itself in the body, the melodrama of petty rivalries, and dealings in money and property. As he rejects the world, he also turns away from Sophie, who has come to embody the burden of profane love and demands of domesticity; their verbal communication falters. Sophie herself can find no language to express her frustration with 'India', and anxiety about the growing distance between Matteo and her.

The second chapter of the novel narrates their long residence at the ashram of the 'Mother'. Language returns as one of the focuses of their disjunct experience and dislocation from each other. In complicating the foreigners' linguistic and discursive experience of 'India', the text enacts a radical shift from literature to orature. Matteo is enraptured by the voice of the 'Mother' from the evening he first hears her speak; it is her voice, rather than the words she speaks, that gives all the 'natural phenomena a wonderful significance', although the narrative, at a later moment, will also incorporate the texts of her speeches. The 'Mother's' aura, emanating from her voice, 'heightens emotion, heightens mood' (*JI* 98), and from the first moment of his intense aural experience, Matteo becomes a disciple and a convert. The inspiration of vocality recalls a similar passage in Hesse's *Siddhartha* on the Buddha's teaching:

> In the evening ... when ... everyone in the camp was alert and gathered together, they heard the Buddha preach. They heard his voice, and this also was perfect, quiet and full of peace. ... The Illustrious One spoke in a soft but firm voice, taught the four main points, taught the Eightfold Path; patiently he covered the usual method of teaching with examples and repetition. Clearly and quietly his voice was carried to his listeners – like a light, like a star in the heavens.
>
> When the Buddha had finished – it was already night – many pilgrims came forward and asked to be accepted into the community.[8]

As each day takes shape as a prolonged wait for the Mother's voice, Matteo abandons his studies, and his conversation with Sophie is abbreviated to monosyllables, or simply breaks down in his wordless attendance on her angry accusations. Though he tries to communicate to Sophie his intense experience, and his conviction that the Mother has opened up for him the true path of enlightenment, 'his words were dead words, they failed to convey the quality of flowering, of the opening of petals and the revealing of a great luminous bloom which was what he experienced that evening' when he first heard the guru speak (*JI* 99).

Jealous of Matteo's total devotion, and unable to reconcile herself to the 'Mother' as competitor or guru, Sophie remains outside the 'Mother's' discourse, in the 'outer world' of physical phenomena from which Matteo has been abstracted. The linguistic politics take a gendered turn in the text's contrast between the 'Mother's' speech, in her conversation with Matteo, when she speaks 'with that sweet lightness of tone that made her seem at times like a young girl' (*JI* 120), and Sophie's bitter and irritated ripostes to her husband. This contrast is augmented by narratorial observations about the 'Mother's' agility and speed, despite her old age, on the badminton court, and Sophie's immobility as she is confined to bed because of a difficult pregnancy. The pregnancy, her first, in turn seems to cause a rift between Matteo and the 'Mother'. On hearing the news about the birth of Matteo and Sophie's son, Giacomo, the 'Mother' says to him, ' "The Monk is becoming a family man, I hear," but she spoke in an uncharacteristically flat, faded tone. She had lost much of her archness, her youthfulness. She seemed distracted' (*JI* 144). While Sophie's resentment against the 'Mother' as rival for Matteo is narrated in detail, the text is much more subtle – or reticent – and ambivalent in the representation of the 'Mother' herself, specifically in the suggestions of profane love in her attitude and behaviour towards Matteo. This ambivalence about the 'Mother' haunts the narrative, not only in this chapter, but also in the next chapter, chapter 3, when Sophie goes on a journey retracing the 'Mother's' early years before she became the guru venerated by a multitude of disciples. If spiritual revelation for Matteo is to be found in the 'Mother's' quotidian presence and preaching, Sophie is equally determined to discover and reveal the mundane truth of her worldly past; Sophie's revelation of the truth about the 'Mother' is pitched against the 'Mother' as the source of revelatory truth to Matteo. The text enacts a complicated dialogue on the human experience of truth and in truth, and the mutual engagements and entanglements of worldly and spiritual truth.

In finding the 'Mother', Matteo's physical journey appears to have come to an end; he has, as it were, finally arrived. While life has now clearly revealed itself as life in the spirit, the ashram is home, place, 'India'. The reversal between Pat and David, which fuels the narrative of 'Scholar and Gypsy', is once more implemented as a textual strategy that enables the movement of *Journey to Ithaca*. In its textual play on the semantics of world and spirit, the profane and the sacred, and in its series of reversals and ironies, *Journey to Ithaca* can be seen as Desai's most crafted narrative to date. In chapter 3, Sophie emerges out of Matteo's shadow into her own narrative. Unable to persuade Matteo to leave the ashram, she leaves with Giacomo, and a second child, Isabel, for Europe. But this journey of return is only the beginning of her own quest for truth, a quest motivated by a two-fold belief in the profanity of the 'Mother' and the sanctity of the love between her and Matteo. Interestingly, her point of departure involves a turning away from her own maternity, for she leaves the children behind with Matteo's parents, and the text resonates with the irony of the transactions when she arrives at motherhood only to depart in order to seek the origins of the 'Mother'. In this respect, her contest with the 'Mother' oscillates between a woman's experience in the world as mistress and lover, and as mother. In a further ironical twist, her journey, which exemplifies her implicit commitment to worldly love, is mapped onto the 'Mother's' quest, through the world, as the young woman Laila, for the guru called 'The Master'.

In chapter 3, the narrative of Laila is interspersed with episodes on Sophie's journey, which retraces Laila's passage to 'Motherhood' from her early days in Alexandria as the child of an Egyptian father and French mother: the young woman Laila leaving her natal home in Alexandria to go to Paris and New York State, all the time restless and longing for spiritual enlightenment; her arrival in India and long residence in India as a foreigner who fails to find social acceptance. As Sophie tells the narrative of the 'Mother', she becomes the 'Mother's' shadow, making a kind of latter-day pilgrimage of her own which displaces Matteo's quest from the novel. Ironically, she is the 'Mother's' true disciple, the one who follows – literally – in the guru's footsteps towards an ecstatic epiphany. This vision is inscribed in the 'Mother's' diary which Sophie manages to get hold of, and which she alone reads. It is the 'Mother's' words, as they are recorded in the diary, which close the main narrative. Sophie has implicitly given up her place, allowing the 'Mother's' voice, which she has so far mediated, to speak in the first person:

> The wind blew about me, and there was music in it as it played upon the harps and lyres of the trees around me. Other than that, there was silence. Out of that silence, a cry. A long, piercing cry that went through my breast like a sword. A great eagle soared forth out of an invisible crevice in the rocks, spreading its wings and floating out into space, launching itself into the unknown to search. With it, my soul too set out in quest ... I began to dance in ecstasy, the ecstasy of knowing my time had come ...
>
> He heard me, my Lord and beloved ... Seeing him, I cried: O, you have come to save me! (*JI* 298, 302)

Nature and woman chorus their mutual turmoil; the body's restlessness is ritualized in the dance of ecstasy. The 'Mother'

81

finds a companionship which the narrative, in the spectacle of the Master's appearance, refuses to bracket off as other-worldly: a metaphysical experience which also implicitly dramatizes the interpenetration of the world of the profane and that of the spiritual. Matteo's enlightenment is not narrated in the novel; he disappears from the ashram after the 'Mother' dies, and ends as an absence known only through Sophie's tenacious quest for him. Determinism, in the journey, has been transformed into self-determination. But in Sophie's firmness there is also resignation, and an ineluctable sense of life as voyage, not merely symbolically but materially, in the world of profane love and human community.

In Matteo, Sophie, and the 'Mother', *Journey to Ithaca* embodies the foreigner as social marginal in India who secures his or her social place ironically by experiencing 'India' as a spiritual quest. In doing so, Desai has not turned away from social reality or the phenomenal world: *Journey to Ithaca*, like her other novels, maps India as place, and if the perspective of mapping is not indigenous, that is precisely the point from which she imagines the vista of how 'India' might appear to the world outside of it, a world whose cognition and recognition have been shaped by a literary discourse of which she herself – as Eurasian but also, importantly, as creative writer – is a legatee. The turn away from indigenous characters in *Journey to Ithaca* is the corollary of the movement of narrative locations outside India. The short stories and novels which precede *In Custody* and which I discussed earlier represent and narrate the world *of* India; *Baumgartner's Bombay* and *Journey to Ithaca* map the world *in* India. This double trajectory implements Desai's fictional journey through the tribulations of human existence, a journey that Hesse himself, and indeed Tagore – another strong literary precursor, as we shall see in the next chapter – had travelled. In concluding 'Remembrance of India', Hesse says, 'this little, age-old platitude – that over and beyond the boundaries of nations and the quarters of the globe there is humanity – this for me was the last and greatest reward of the journey'.[9] And to quote Desai again: 'The subject of all my books has been what Ortega y Gasset called "the terrors of facing, single-handed, the ferocious assaults of existence."'[10] In narrating the daily life of ordinary Indian characters, or the metaphysical aspirations of foreign

82

voyagers, Desai has been true to the professed 'subject' of her fiction. She has not succumbed to the seductions of a universalism that transcends cultural and national differences, but in locating her main characters, Indian or foreign, in their own realistic and realistically particular histories, she shows how their journeys through the commonalities of human tribulation begin and proceed through differences that are as intrinsic to their co-presence in a fictional community as the trials they share.

5

Home, World

Fasting, Feasting, Anita Desai's latest novel, is the companion piece to *Clear Light of Day*. In *Fasting, Feasting,* Desai returns to the Indian family, and the relations between parents and children. Parental neglect is frequently referred to in *Clear Light of Day*, but the novel focuses on the children's shared experience of neglect which both bonds and divides them. Neglect – and rejection – as the condition of everyday experience and the frame of a life-long existence, is the burden of *Fasting, Feasting*. The daughter, Uma, in *Fasting, Feasting* bears shades of both Bim and Tara; like Bim, she is the one who did not get away but she has none of Bim's autonomy. In the novel, she is the household drudge doing her parents' bidding as Tara does her husband's, but her domestic bondage far exceeds Tara's for her parents have never thought her worthy of attention or encouragement. In her absence of self-worth, Uma's predicament is an extreme magnification of the discomfiting insecurity that Tara clearly feels in being marginalized in the family. Beginning with what she has left unsaid in *Clear Light of Day*, Desai, in her latest novel, paints an unforgiving picture of the psychological havoc which parents wreak on their children. *Fasting, Feasting* is a novel unsparing in its detail of parental abuse, and the children's self-abuse which is the tragic consequence.

While Part 1 of the novel, set in India, details Uma's subjection to her parents, and her frustrated and pathos-ridden attempts at self-fashioning, Part 2 moves to suburban United States, and the experience of Uma's brother, Arun, in an equally dysfunctional American family. The changes in location align with the globalizing orientations of *Baumgartner's Bombay* and *Journey to Ithaca*; so too does the determinism which haunts

Desai's characters and which she traces to their early life. In *Fasting, Feasting*, the dysfunctional family returns as the main site of fictional exploration, specifically in the parents' use and abuse of authority as they withhold their love. The novel inscribes Desai's most stringent critique of parental failure; there is almost no redeeming feature in the characterization of MamaPapa, that linked identity, or, perhaps more appropriately, entity which is the function of absolute self-interest. In emptying them of kindness, Desai also embodies in them the most oppressive legacies of patriarchal subjection of women, and the material and status obsessions of the modern Indian middle class. They are an unattractive combination; in being unnamed, MamaPapa seems devoid not only of parental nurture but of finer human qualities.

In her introduction to Tagore's children's play *The Post Office*, Desai observes:

> Tagore knew imprisonment as a child – the imprisonment of the spirit. One of his earliest memories was of a servant called Shyam who would 'place me in a selected spot, trace a chalk line around me, and warn me with a solemn fact and uplifted finger of the perils of transgressing this circle. Whether the danger was physical or mental I never fully understood, but fear certainly possessed me.' Confined to the immense, gloomy family home in Calcutta, he could only gaze with longing at 'this limitless thing called Outside, flashes, sounds and scents of which used to come and touch me through interstices. It seemed to want to beckon me through the shutters with a variety of gestures. But it was free and I was bound – there was no way of our meeting.' In poem after poem he wrote of this sense of imprisonment, balanced by an instinctive awareness of the possibility of release.[1]

This passage is worth quoting in full because, while it speaks of Tagore, it also points directly to Desai's own fictional pre-occupations. As we have seen, Desai's novels represent characters bound to lives which they did not choose to lead but which they are powerless to change, and from which they can rarely escape. Home, for many of them, is prison, the location of their fragile self-identity, and the ground on which that identity is bruised, battered, and voided of meaning in the practice of everyday life. If Tagore as a child feels himself in prison, Desai's characters enact in fiction how such a sense of imprisonment, and the psychological trauma it effects, become the matrix that consciously or unconsciously drives their actions, forms their choices, and shapes their self-identities as adults and social relations. 'Home' is the prison lodged within the deepest reaches of the human psyche, and being 'at home' means searching for an adult accommodation to the ineluctable condition of imprisonment. Some of Desai's characters remember, like Tagore, the child's gaze on the 'Outside', that magical and transformative space of autonomy and agency, and these glimpses of the possible through the 'interstices' of desire activate their struggle for 'release' from their allocated places and identities. In *Fasting, Feasting*, these glimpses, as they occur to Uma in India and her brother, Arun, in the United States, are few and far between.

Fasting, feasting: in the novel, the two terms are sequential, opposed, discrete but also conjoined, and through their complex semantic and metaphorical associations, Desai drives home her critique of the hunger for social status, and rapacious appetite for consumption, which define the bourgeois family that overarches the locational distance of India and the United States. Absorbed in each other, MamaPapa are not simply ogrish in themselves; they are consumers of their own children, and at the centre of the network of the extended Indian family where consumption, in its different forms and manifestations, becomes the single most important bond that displaces all other kinship feelings. Taken forcibly away from school in order to become the nurse of her sister, Aruna, and later her brother, Arun, Uma, as the eldest daughter, is the body on which parental self-interest, justified in the daughter's filial duty and obedience, feeds and sustains itself. The body rebels: Uma is prone to epileptic fits which, as they happen unpredictably in front of outsiders and other relations, cause her status-obsessed parents the maximum embarrassment. The novel shows other moments of protest when she joins her despised vagrant Aunt Mira, *Mira-masi*, on an escapade to an ashram, and her cousin Ramu for her first and only meal in a restaurant with her ill-tempered parents. *Mira-masi* arrives from time to time unannounced, and irritates Mama by preparing her own food which Uma delights in, and the ebullient Ramu, castigated as the black sheep of the family, instigates the restaurant outing, where bad food and a satirically portrayed ambience go unnoticed by an entranced Uma on her first experience of dining away from home.

These experiences, in their very depletion, underline the hunger in Uma for the outside world, and accentuate the famished condition of home. Swallowed up by the family, Uma is fascinated by those whom the family has ejected; both Mira and Ramu are uncomfortable reminders to MamaPapa of the organic parts that do not fit into the retentive corporate body, and their return provokes renewed motions of expulsion. Despite Uma's adulation, Mira and Ramu are not embodied in their own narratives. They arrive unexpectedly, out of nowhere, and the vantage of the narrative when they appear is on their bewildering existence, cut off from the regimen of the family, in the wilderness of an outside world. While Uma's adulation draws attention to their ex-centricity, the novel stops far short of a full disclosure of their presence in alternative worlds outside of home. They disappear from the family narrative, never to be seen again, and what happens to them circulates as family gossip and rumour. As symptoms of dysfunction, they are suppressed, and in this suppression, the extended family survives in its self-illusion as an evolving social organism. They have removed themselves from the family body and corporate narrative, and, if in the past their periodical reappearances provoked discomfort and necessitated expurgation, their final disappearance paradoxically refuels the family in its complacent morality of necessary waste in order to ensure corporate health and survival.

The novel shows repeatedly MamaPapa, and all the relatives of their generation, not only as incapable of any insight into the condition of their existence, but thoroughly interpellated by a corporate ideology of respectability that, in the end, works against the family's continued survival into the next generation. Mira and Ramu may be unlamented, but the family is diminished in the loss of its members, and the family's suicidal self-consumption is nowhere more apparent than in the experience of Anamika, Uma's cousin. Anamika has no voice in the novel; what we see of her is entirely mediated by the older generation's approving gaze in which she appears as the perfect embodiment of the ideal daughter and familial asset. Pretty, polite, and willing to please, Anamika is from childhood Uma's binary other, the one who will grow up to fulfil the family's expectations of an attractive marital prospect, uphold the family's social reputation, and ensure its respect among the aggregate of bourgeois families that count for community in the novel. A success at school where Uma is a failure, Anamika is accepted as a scholarship student at Oxford University, and although, as a woman, the possibility of a scholarly future for her never figures in the family's calculations, the letter of acceptance itself is treasured, and becomes a dowry item when she is eventually married.

Anamika's silence is symbolic of her erasure as an individual; her story can only be heard through the family's narrative of itself, and as it takes a tragic turn, the details of what happen to her, like those that pertain to Mira and Ramu, circulate as fragments in a family text designed to suppress their true and devastating import. We hear rumours of abuse by her mother-in-law, and hints of collective violence by her husband's family, but they are represented by MamaPapa and other relatives as nothing but malicious gossip designed to damage the family in the eyes of society. When Anamika fails to turn up at Aruna's wedding, her own parents present the absence as a sign that she is so valued by her marital family that she cannot be allowed out of their sight, and her failure to visit her parental home even once after her marriage is justified in similar terms. These justifications are, in turn, endorsed by MamaPapa and other relatives. What the narrative foregrounds is the family's conspiracy of silence as symptomatic of a collective pathology that will avert its gaze from the torture of its own kind in the interest of its own survival. As it consumes Anamika in its own self-interest, the family becomes, in turn, a self-consuming artefact.

When news arrives that Anamika has been burned alive, there are various speculations in the neighbourhood about a suicide, an accident, or that she has been deliberately set alight by her own mother-in-law and husband. The family summons its defences and – in an ultimate suppression of Anamika's identity and claims not only as an individual but as a member of the corporate body – it refuses to involve itself in ascertaining the truth. Uma's continued survival in abjection is momentarily de-centred by the matter-of-fact statements on Anamika's life-long suffering and death:

Anamika was forty-five years old that year, two years older than her [Uma]. She had been married for twenty-five years, the twenty-five years that Uma had not. Now she is dead, a jar of grey ashes. Uma, clasping her knees, can feel that she is still flesh, not ashes. But she feels like ash – cold colourless, motionless ash. (*FF* 152)

If, through Anamika, Desai is drawing attention to the woman's unspeakable bondage within the marital home, she does so with tact but also devastating innuendo. Typifying this restraint, the statistics, or hard facts, of Anamika's life and marriage underline but do not dramatize her suffering. Yet what is left unspoken, in that it points to the extent, in terms of duration, of what she has had to endure, intensifies the horror of a hardly imaginable – and barely representable – suffering of a woman slowly consumed alive and finally incinerated on the bonfire of the family's bourgeois vanities. It makes Uma's spinsterhood seem for a moment benign, until we see that, for her, to 'feel' alive in the flesh is to 'feel' this flesh, as 'ash', in its final dissolution. The family has put a premium on its material comfort and survival, and its corporate body is a body without feeling. Anamika is the body in pain, and her lingering death-in-life which ends in the extreme pain of being burned alive can only be recognized by Uma through her own feeling body. Uma's belated recognition of her identity with Anamika represents the only kinship and social accommodation that their lives within the family have to offer. As the site of emotions, Uma's body struggles beyond its own incarceration to reach out to a once feeling body, now beyond pain, and this movement outside suggests a redemptive humanity which continues unextinguished despite life-long adversity, and which we shall see in further instances later on in this chapter. Uma may not be able to grow away from MamaPapa, but glimpses of what is possible outside lie within her to compose the narrative's fragile counter-discourse to the prison-house of family.

Anamika does not, or cannot, take the step outside of 'home'; neither does Aruna, the family's other prized marital prospect who turns out to be the true inheritor of the values of consumption. After her marriage into a prosperous Bombay family, Aruna leaves her natal home in the provincial town for the metropolis, and her life there as an avid consumer, characterized by shopping and parties, is reported in letters designed to emphasize MamaPapa's shabby gentility. On a rare home-visit, she is hypercritical of everything she feels she has left behind, to the extent that even Papa, 'not easily shaken in his profound conviction of his status and authority, seemed uneasy and sat upright and conversed instead of scowling into space as was his habit and one from which no one in the family had ever tried to pry him loose' (*FF* 108–9). Aruna suffers the insatiable hunger of materialist desire, and Uma, as she watches her sister 'vexed to the point of tears' because neither her parental nor her marital home can meet her demands, 'felt pity for her' (*FF* 109). Here again, we glimpse Uma's sympathetic imagination, which her own life-long exile from sympathy cannot destroy, but she can only observe Aruna's frustration in silence, and her sibling feeling is too habituated to the discipline of Papa's 'status and authority' to challenge or bring fundamental change to the unhomeliness of the home in which she is placed.

In the novel, there are three moments when Mama is temporarily detached from Papa, and she and Uma reach some kind of understanding. The first of these moments is when they share a laugh at Aruna's fashionable haircut; the second when Mama tries to urge an intransigent Papa to allow Uma to consult a specialist about her weakening eyesight; the last, which I shall discuss in greater detail later, when they join the rituals for Anamika's river burial. Each of these moments develops around the body, its function, dysfunction, and dissolution, and, to borrow Tagore's words, they 'beckon...through the shutters with a variety of gestures', but they remain gestures, bound to their own transience, and their transformative impact on the social order of the family remains unnarrated. If 'home' is embodied, the body's mode and space of extension in the novel is severely curtailed. Affiliation is replaced by the consumption of one self by the corporate body of family, and when this feasting is done, what is disgorged survives as fragments which, in Aruna, are reconstituted as a self defined by an insatiable and inchoate frustration about incompleteness – nothing at 'home' can be good enough for her, as she materializes into the virulent consumer who turns on her parental and marital hosts. In Uma, fragments of the self survive in abjection – a daily and continuous fast disrupted by moments of struggle for the satisfaction of self-meaning and self-expression.

For Arun, the move to the United States transports the body onto foreign soil but 'home' is lodged in the body's physical constitution. As the only son and male heir, he is the focus of his father's aspirations, the proof of Mama's fulfilment of her obligations as wife, and guarantee of her status in a patriarchal lineage. He enjoys the advantages of education which Uma is deprived of; masculinity, however, is a very double-edged privilege. From an early age, Arun enjoys Papa's excessive attention, and is subjected to an unrelenting regimen of schoolwork and a meat-eating diet. The narrative, focalized through Uma as observer, shows the full impression of this upbringing upon his physical appearance:

> All the years of scholarly toil had worn down any distinguishing features Arun's face might once have had. They had left the essentials: a nose, eyes, mouth, ears. But he held his lips tightly together, his nose was as flattened as could possibly be, and his eyes were shielded by the thick glasses his relentless studies had necessitated. There was nothing else – not the hint of a smile, frown, laugh or anything: these had all been ground down till they had disappeared. This blank face now stared at the letter [from the American university] and faced another phase of his existence arranged for him by Papa. (*FF* 121)

The only resistance we see is in Arun's refusal of meat from childhood, and, in the east-coast American university where he studies, his disinterest in food is matched by his apathy to his surroundings, his roommate and other students, and his fellow countrymen. Apparently affectless, Arun recalls Baumgartner in his crab-like existence as he scuttles between classes and dormitory, carefully avoiding all but the most perfunctory human contact. Escape from home means the freedom of total anonymity and to eschew any form of social engagement which entails obligation; this, tragically, is what singularity has come to mean for Arun. The last third of the novel narrates his life in suburban America, especially the summer he spends with the Pattons, and it is here, in the midst of another seriously dysfunctional family, that a fragile individuality emerges.

In the American chapters, food and its ancillary activities – shopping, cooking, eating, digesting, regurgitation – are much more explicitly foregrounded in the narrative organization. Each of the American characters is defined by their attitude and association with food: Mr Patton's virility is expressed in his habit of cooking large steaks on the barbecue and consuming them semi-raw; Mrs Patton, a well-meaning but completely witless woman, comes into her own only when she trundles her trolley around the supermarket, piling it high with products for a family larder that is always already full with what the family cannot consume; Rod, the son, eats to support an endless fitness regime, and in the daughter Melanie's bulimia, the replacement of nurture by feeding, and kinship by an artificial network of provision and consumption issues in a pathological condition that is as inarticulate as it is melodramatic in its denunciation.

As cultural critique, the American chapters, in their exclusive focus on food, consumption and waste, appear much less nuanced than the Indian narrative. However, it is possible to argue that, underpinning the attack on the most observable materialist obsessions of suburban America, it is the inhabitation of family in Arun, and the exploration of what transformative possibilities being abroad might bring, which is the real burden of the last third of the narrative. In other words, Arun in America is both 'at home' and 'foreign' – or in the 'world' – and the two terms, as in Desai's other novels, are thrown open to the scrutiny of each other, as they coexist paradoxically in identity and difference. Like Uma, Arun is observant though uncommunicative, and through his silent comments on the Pattons, his self-identity takes shape as unyielding difference which defies the best efforts of Mrs Patton to draw him in. This recalcitrance, which remains invisible within his own family, defines his American sojourn; ironically, being alien protects him from the all-consuming menace of 'home', and enables a mediated freedom in alienation. What the humanity is which can be recovered or retrieved, and how Arun discovers the possible extension of the self beyond the impositions of family, mark his story as they do Uma's. But in Arun's case, the life-long experience of love withheld interacts with his privileged position in patriarchy to disable and paralyse him. Near the end of the novel, on a family outing, as he comes upon Melanie in the midst of a degrading bulimic attack, he

> backs away. He stands, his hands twisted at his sides, looking around to see if any help is coming. But the woods hold out nothing... 'Melanie,' he says desperately, 'shall I call your mother?'

Staring at her, huddled on the ground and trembling, he feels this could be a scene in a film – a maiden at the feet of the hero crying – but of course it is no such thing ... [T]his is a real pain and a real hunger. But what hunger does a person so sated feel? He croaks, 'Shall I, Melanie, shall I?' but is rooted to the spot, its reality holds him captive. There is no escape, and it is Mrs Patton who comes in search of them and finds them. (*FF* 225)

There is an inarticulateness and helplessness about Arun which contrast with Uma as she feels Aruna's frustration or Anamika's horrifying end. Desai does not play up the gender issue but, equally, it is no mere coincidence that the son of the family, confronted with a young woman – his contemporary – in need, shows a distress that is as much an expression of his inadequate masculinity as a failure of fellow feeling. While Arun's helplessness suggests the incapacities of sympathy, the narrative of Uma's responses resonates with better promise in excess of the occasion of sympathy. Beyond difference and alienation as self-identification, Desai, in *Fasting, Feasting*, explores the possibilities of humanity under the most adverse of circumstances. Such adversities need not be, as in *Baumgartner's Bombay*, the fallout of epic world history; the fact that they exist in the everyday lives of families brings them more intensely and perspicaciously close to 'home'.

Earlier in this chapter, I have referred to Desai's introduction to Tagore's *The Post Office*. For Desai, Tagore is not simply the incidental occasion for a moment of self-reference. In previous chapters, I have drawn attention to some of the references to Tagore's songs and their symbolic figurations in Desai's stories and novels. There is an undeniable sense that, with Tagore, Desai feels a special community as a writer. In her essay 'Rereading Tagore', she writes,

When Tagore was alive, he travelled constantly and his ghost is still a restless one as if it were in search, in true ghostly tradition, of something that had been mislaid and needed to be found again, or remained unfinished and sought fulfilment. Would it be worth our while today to join that search, I wonder.[2]

The traces of Tagore in Desai's own writing suggest the presence of a literary predecessor that does not amount to an inhabitation, and yet is more haunting than specific quotations or invocations of poems and songs to punctuate moments of narrative drama. As the article reveals, Desai challenges the reception of Tagore as a mystic by modernist writers like Yeats and Pound who, earlier in the twentieth century, enthused about his collection of poems *Gitanjali*. To Desai, this is a 'misinterpretation', and is largely why, after the first flush of enthusiasm, both Tagore and his work have 'been thrown on the dust-heap along with turn-of-the-century Orientalism, theosophy, Madame Blavatsky, Fitzgerald's Omar Khayyám and Schopenhauer's philosophy'.[3] In her own fictional work, and in her rereading of Tagore and introductions to a number of recent reprints of his work, Desai seeks to relocate Tagore the realist, engaged through his poetry with the miseries, 'the squalor and sorrow' of modern life in India, and whose prose style and stories are 'uncompromisingly realistic and expose uncomfortable truths about society and its systems'.[4] In reorienting the reception of Tagore, Desai stresses his commitment to the reform of civil society that not only exceeds the nationalistic frames of his own anti-colonial times but has enduring relevance to our own contemporary, postcolonial age.

Rather than transporting the reader to a transcendent realm, which is how Tagore's verse has been read by his western readers, Desai demonstrates that the lyricism of Tagore's songs articulate the language of imagination as difference in a world that seems entirely imprisoned in its own corruptions – a language of transformation that speaks of beauty, love, and truth in the longings of the heart that coordinates with the discourse of the social reformer. In Tagore's writing, Desai reads the indissociable connections and contest between the languages of reality and imagination, and the discourses of human bondage and freedom they signify. These are the languages and discourses of Desai's own fiction, the mapping of a search which she also sees in Tagore, and through which the 'mislaid' tradition of Tagore finds a contemporary haunting, if not exactly a home.

From the rich profusion of Tagore's *Gitanjali*, no. XXIV offers a small but not unrepresentative instance of his lyrical and imagistic resonance:

> If the day is done, if birds sing no more, if the wind has flagged tired, then draw the veil of darkness thick upon me, even as thou hast

wrapt the earth with the coverlet of sleep and tenderly closed the petals of the drooping lotus at dusk.

From the traveller, whose sack of provisions is empty before the voyage is ended, whose garment is torn and dust-laden, whose strength is exhausted, remove shame and poverty, and renew his life like a flower under the cover of thy kindly night.[5]

The poems of *Gitanjali* are variously addressed to a source of power, a godhead outside the self, alternately male or feminized, and embodied in figures of the beloved. This power is manifest in nature as nurture and the space of recuperation from human vicissitude, as we can see from the actions of the invisible hand of night in the above poem that wraps the earth in sleep, closes the lotus petals at dusk, and soothes and renews the exhausted traveller. It is also in nature that the first person speaker finds the transformative space where the daily realities of pain can seek not only release and comfort, but poetic deliverance, as we can see in no. LXXXIV:

It is the pang of separation that spreads throughout the world and gives birth to shapes innumerable in the infinite sky.

It is this sorrow of separation that gazes in silence all night from star to star and becomes lyric among rustling leaves in rainy darkness of July.

It is this overspreading pain that deepens into loves and desires, into sufferings and joys in human homes; and this it is that ever melts and flows in songs through my poet's heart.[6]

If the earlier poem attributes the power of transformation to an external source, in this poem, it is human pain and sorrow that first trangress the boundaries of the self, and 'give birth' to, or reinvent, the visual perceptions and aural rhythms of nature. The repetitive openings of the three stanzas suggest an imaginative – and generative – process that is continuous, repeated, and repeatable, but also highly charged and all-encompassing, in its ability to cross fluently from the infinitude of the sky to the minute movements of the rain rustling the leaves in the summer night. In the final stanza, pain returns to the world of human reality, its origins in the self, and its abode in the primary community of the 'home'. In this return, it is no longer pure debilitation, but the point of departure for the excavation of the intensities of 'love and desires' and other 'sufferings and joys'. Rather than speak of defeat, it is discomposed – 'melts' – channelled, and translated into the poet's creative agency.

In Desai's writing, as in Tagore's, nature offers the rich diversity of images as well as regular patterns through which human realities and change can be figured, symbolized, and represented. The aestheticization of nature often carries an environmental imperative, for it is also in nature, and through reconnecting with nature, that human reality might be borne, and the change of perspective crucial to transforming self and world can be possible. We have seen both these processes from the beginning in 'Studies in the Park', 'Surface Textures', 'Scholar and Gypsy', and *Fire on the Mountain,* and more recently in the ecstasy of the Mother in *Journey to Ithaca.* It is there also in *Fasting, Feasting.* One of the temporary moments of relief from parental tyranny which Uma enjoys in the novel is when she visits an ashram with *Mira-masi.* Outside their spartan room,

> stood an earthern jar of drinking water. Every morning the water carrier would fill it with water from the river below, down at the edge of a path that twisted through the scrub and rocks of the low dun hills, across the sand to the riverbed where a narrow green channel of water ran between parched clay. Enormous fishing eagles circled languidly in the sky above the still landscape. Only during the morning and evening prayers was there a beating of cymbals and ringing of bells and a coming together of people on the temple precincts. For the rest of the day there was silence... Uma was perfectly happy not to be noticed. She had never been more unsupervised or happier in her life. (*FF* 57)

The activities among which Uma finds herself are both human and natural, and what is emphasized, in a characteristic Desai descriptive, is their interconnection and harmony. Uma is not part of it; if she feels more at home in the ashram than she has ever felt in her life with her parents, this homeliness is not warranted, but what is significant – and poignant – is that just the fact of being physically present as an observer can be the cause of such rare and complete content. The hostile realities of Uma's world are temporarily displaced by another reality that enables her to glimpse, for the first time, an unwitting desire and an experience of the possible. These moments are few and far between in Uma's life. In the next encounter, she is on the river with Aruna's wedding party: 'Everyone was in a state of high excitement', the women especially, and 'Uma, thrilled by this licence, simply sprang off the prow and plunged in without hesitation, as if this were what she had been preparing to do all her life.' Dragged out of the water, she has to apologize to Aruna for spoiling the party, but she knows that

> when she had plunged into the dark water and let it close quickly and tightly over her ... [i]t was not fear she felt, or danger. Or, rather, these were only what edged something much darker, wilder, more thrilling, a kind of exultation – it was exactly what she had always wanted, she realised. Then they had saved her. The saving was what made her shudder and cry, there on the sandbar, soaking wet, while the morning sun leapt up in the hazy, sand-coloured sky and struck the boat, the brass pots that the women held, and their white drifting garments in the water. (*FF* 110–11)

Unpremeditated, Uma's plunge into the river speaks of her unconscious desire for union with what she can only observe as an outsider; in psychoanalytic terms, the death-wish is plain for all to see, but what is also significant, in the narrative context of the novel, is Uma's total lack of concern for those anxieties about risk and hazard that afflict adult deliberations, and the imperative of individual desire which, at least for a moment, shakes free of the unrelenting superego that MamaPapa embodies. That she ends up relegated once again to the position of the outsider – as she was in the ashram – watching but excluded from the habitat of the women in the morning sun, is consistent with her narrative, and typifies Desai's representation of a subject for whom the accidents of history constitute a life-long bondage to a set of social circumstances that demand and extract total abjection. Her gaze is the gaze of Baumgartner watching the women fenced off by the barbed wire of the internment camp, her tears the expression of the distress which Desai's stronger women – Nanda and Bim among them – cannot shed, and which cries out to be heard in the very mediated narrative of Anamika. How can the voice of the subaltern woman be heard, Giyatri Chakravarty Spivak once asked in a seminal article.[7] To follow up on this question, how can a bourgeois woman like Anamika who is imprisoned within the family's complicity of silence, and ultimately sacrificed on the bonfire of bourgeois vanities, be heard? I shall return to this question later on in this chapter.

At the end of Part 1, Uma is among the family party gathered for the ritual immersion of Anamika's ashes in the river. MamaPapa and the older generation, usually so vocal in opinion and command, are silent and bowed; the only voice is that of 'a lapwing on the bank that is crying frantically, over and over'. 'Did-you-do-it?' it cries. 'Did-you, did-you, did-you-do-it?' (*FF* 155). If nature sounds the suppressed voice of human conscience, the narrative suggests the return of those kinship feelings that have been so long displaced from the family. On the journey back to the shore, Uma finds her mother's hand clasping hers tightly, and she 'squeezes the hand back, thinking, they are together still, they have the comfort of each other ... [I]t is a bond' (*FF* 155–6). What is significant here is not so much the mother's need – we have seen the imperatives of such need all through the narrative – but its admission and physical expression, and more importantly, the ability of Uma to respond despite the harshness of her life-long exile from her mother's care and affection. Her agency is redefined: she may not be able to change her life and her circumstances, but she is unembittered, and her continued capacity for love, and to love, signals a self that remains true to – is at home in – its essential humanity. In the final moment, she 'dips her jar in the river, and lifts it high over her head. When she tilts it and pours it out, the murky water catches the blaze of the sun and flashes fire' (*FF* 156). She becomes, in this moment, one of the women on the river-bank whose daily activities she could only watch on the earlier occasion of the wedding party. In her own private ritual – a kind of libation to the dead – the poetic images that conclude her narrative also suggest an expression, or outpouring, of the redemptive love that can offer an unexpected transformative point of view – a flash of brilliance – on both the environment and the self. If the world of human vicissitude is defined by transience, it is at moments of illumination such as this that time as grinding repetition is disrupted, and that the legacy of Tagore's vision of the 'overspreading pain ... that ever melts and flows in songs through my poet's heart'[8] is relocated in Desai's writing.

As I have pointed out in the discussion of *Clear Light of Day*, critics have expressed uneasiness about the ending of the novel, and detected larger social issues at stake that exceed the resolution of individual circumstance in narrative closure. There is no doubt that social inequality and injustice, oppression and exclusion continue to vex and provoke Desai, and her novels return again and again to their dehumanizing practices in different places but especially within the everyday experience and interactions of family and small communities in which she sees most Indian lives are lived. While there is no doubting the insight and illuminative power of Desai's critique of India through the detailed lives of its individual inhabitants, what seems to be left unsaid in her fiction is the articulation between individual and social transformation. This articulation is another vantage on the self and others, inside and outside, home and the world – those binary terms which Desai's novels have done so much to critique, disrupt, and reconfigure in a multiplicity of relations that take into account their transgressions, crossings, and possible interconnections. In this context, the first issue that arises in our exploration of Desai as social critic in the rest of this chapter is necessarily that of her apparent silence on the place of individual transformation and agency in the larger arena of social reform.

Another related issue is the place of her fictional subjects in the social hierarchies of Indian society – or class – in Desai's fiction. In Coetzee's comments on *Journey to Ithaca* quoted in the previous chapter, he perceives a turn away from those on 'the extreme margins of society, the defeated for whom there is no social recourse or recompense' to 'the vicissitudes of a pair of well-to-do, spoiled European hippies'.[9] If Coetzee is right, then not only can the middle-class woman not speak, but furthermore, her experience cannot be worth speaking of. These comments seem even more questionable in the light of Coetzee's own fictional trajectory from Michael K to the protagonist of *Disgrace* who can hardly be considered a social marginal. However, it is pointless to turn these comments into an occasion for a slanging match. To take this argument in another and more fruitful direction, it is true that most of Desai's fictional subjects are of bourgeois origins, even if their place ranges across the broad extent of the so-called middle class, from the relative prosperity of Nanda Kaul to a low-ranking professional like Deven, and their social descent, as in the case of Baumgartner, is marked in the narrative. None of these subjects can be said to suffer from genuine material privation; in other words, their individual, and often tragic, predicament springs from cultural displacements to which socio-economic inequities contribute, but which they cannot really account for. Rather than being the function of economic hardship, marginality in Desai's novels delivers a trenchant critique of the social injustice which lies hidden within bourgeois culture as it is systematized in ritual and everyday practices, and justified in inherited cultural orthodoxies.

In her study of the plot formation of novels by 'elite' Indian women writers – including Desai – Rosemary Marangoly George observes how 'the related Indian histories of nationalism, of the "Hindu way of life," of English-language-Indian literature, and of Indian women's movements have worked in unison to establish the unenviable situation that the elite Indian woman finds herself in: she has all the material benefits of home, of consumerism, of leisure and yet finds herself deeply unfulfilled and completely alienated from the roles available to her'.[10] The specific plot which George discusses centres on the *ennui* and frustration of the urban, bourgeois housewife which reaches breaking point in some domestic crisis and forces the protagonist 'to confront the parameters of herself, her life and her worth'[11] before she is either folded back into domesticity, after a period of intense self-examination, or rejects her former life altogether for an unspecified new beginning. While exploring the complex historical and socio-political dynamics of this plot and woman subject formation, George's contention is that the very elite and upper-class status of the women subjects and the lives they lead make them unrepresentative of Indian women or India. Furthermore, 'if we expect this ennui ... which leads ... to the production of written texts, to evolve into a radical political declaration, we will be disappointed'.[12] To George, these women subjects are not only unrepresentative but far too accustomed to their entitlements of social privilege to make resistance against the status quo a viable option and political agency possible.

While George only deals with women subjects, and one text by Desai – *Where Shall We Go This Summer?* – which is hardly representative, her inquiry raises questions about self and social transformation and bourgeois subjectivity that are germane to this discussion. As social critic, Desai perceives the dynamics of history and the changes in the larger social world working through the atomized lives of individual subjects in their families although she seldom refers to the events of this external world directly in her own novels. As history is acted out in everyday life, individuals are social actors participating in history, and in this interaction, the individual's capacity to alter the course of history is grounded upon the transformation he or she effects in his or her own life. In many ways, Desai's reappraisal of Tagore the realist is oriented by a keen concern about this interaction; how social hierarchy acts coercively upon different subjects to empty them out of desire and fix them in their allocated places; and how the struggles within the self and between self and the world enter into each other in the formation of subjects, community, and meaning. My contention is that Desai's rereading of Tagore registers a displacement of her inquiry into social change through individual transformation which also signals her profound unease about 'political declaration' and programmatic political reform in which the terms of individual struggle and agency are often framed. This is another vantage on the return of Tagore in her work; without being explicitly self-referential, her championship of Tagore inscribes her refutation of the recent queries about her privileged fictional subjects which Coetzee and George's comments represent.

In the second part of her essay 'Re-reading Tagore', she discusses Tagore's opposition to the political programme of nationalism of his own time. Tagore, she says, 'worshipped no external deity but the capacity of human beings for love and creativity – for him the Divine was the human imagination. Modern as these ideas of Tagore's were in comparison with Gandhi's, there was one modern idea he would not go along with, and that was nationalism.'[13] Tagore's novel *The Home and the World* (1915) is his most substantial fictional critique of the nationalistic *Swadeshi* movement in Bengal. The title of the novel suggests the conjunction but also the contrary pressures of family and political commitments, the nation as the construct of tradition and of modernity, the contemplative inner life and a life of social and political action. Through a succession of first-person narratives, told by Nikhil, a Hindu and a Maharaja, his wife Bimala, and the *Swadeshi* leader Sandip, the novel maps the contours of a triangulated relationship that begins with Bimala as the self-effacing and reverential wife of Nikhil, and follows her as she takes her first tentative steps out of *purdah* to an outside world, and through to an involvement with Sandip which is both romantic and political. Each of the characters become alternately the focus of the narrative, and the pivot on which the relationship turns in a multiply voiced dialogue about what 'home' and 'world' mean to each of them and how these meanings change in response to external circumstances which, in turn, activate perceptions of the self unknown before.

Though a zamindar and the embodiment of inherited privilege, Nikhil is portrayed on the one hand as the benevolent patron of his tenants and those who serve him, and on the other, as the modernizing subject who encourages Bimala to learn English and wear western dresses, and adopts western technology to enhance the quality and productivity of native craft. In this respect, his practice at home is consistent with that in the world he governs, and tradition and modernity find a place in both domains. He is also unconcerned about money, possession, and his own comforts, but rather than being the function of assumed wealth and privilege, the novel represents him as the *exemplum* of the contemplative ideal and the thoroughly examined life. What distinguishes him is his inwardness, and his inner probings grow in depth and intensity as Bimala's 'stepping out' fuels his examination of a self defined in terms of his role as her lord and husband. 'I was never self-conscious,' he admits. 'But nowadays I often try to take an outside view – to see myself as Bimal sees me.' (*HW* 64) In this comment, we see the movement from and between a subjective and objective vantage on the self as one of the multiple trangressions of 'home' and 'world' that Tagore enacts in the novel.

From the start, Nikhil appears epicene, and is characterized as womanly, even by his wife, and this effeminacy, coordinated with paternalistic benevolence, contemplation, and other-worldliness, stands in contrast with the masculinist Sandip, identified by his sensuous desire, materialist covetousness, and political ambition. 'Every man has a natural right to possess,' Sandip declares unambiguously, 'and therefore greed is natural ... Nature surrenders herself, but only to the robber. For she delights in this forceful desire, this forceful abduction ...

What I desire, I desire positively, superlatively. I want to knead it with both my hands and both my feet; I want to smear it all over my body; I want to gorge myself to the full' (*HW* 45–6). His seduction of Bimala shows a calculated premeditation but also an unexpected hesitancy: 'The passage from the narrow to the larger world is stormy. When [Bimala] is familiar with this freedom, then I shall know where my place is. If I discover I do not fit in with the arrangement of the outer world, then I shall not quarrel with my fate, but silently take my leave ...'(*HW* 57–8). In these two quotations, we get a glimpse of the complexity of Sandip's characterization; his chauvinistic and rapacious desire, which is palpably physical, is tempered by a consciousness of his intersubjective relations vis-à-vis Bimala, and that his 'place' in the 'outer world' is contingent upon her departure from 'home'. As the narrative goes on to show, Bimala's progressive crossings from 'home' to the 'world' provoke a greater consciousness in Sandip of his own motives, and the justification, beyond the drives of appetite, of his own nationalistic project. To him, she is no mere object of sexual desire; in her, he fashions the image of a maternal deity, a goddess who is also the symbol of mother-nation. He justifies his project of invention in two ways: through an appeal to a sceptical philosophical tradition which postulates untruth as the only truth, contra to truth as an ideal to be pursued which he sees as Nikhil's motivation, and which he despises; and an apprehension of the Bengali character:

> Who says 'Truth shall Triumph?' Delusion shall win in the end. The Bengali understood this when he conceived the image of the ten-handed goddess astride her lion, and spread her worship in the land. Bengal must now create a new image to enchant and conquer the world. *Bande Mataram*! (*HW* 125)

Nationalist politics, as it is embodied in Sandip, has a material base, not in the economic realities of colonial Bengal, but in the worldliness lodged at the core of its leader that issues as voracious appetite for possession and power, and functions on its appeal to the xenophobia of Bengalis on one hand, and their cultural inheritances in superstition and animistic beliefs on the other. It is a powerful configuration of essential human drives and tactical manoeuvring that is foregrounded by the highly charged and mobile energies that distinguish the rhetoric of

103

Sandip's narrative self-revelations, and comments on his actions by other characters. As he penetrates deeper and deeper into Nikhil's household – signified by his crossing over into the boundaries of the woman's quarter at one point in the novel – he enforces a dual movement in Nikhil: inwardly into a re-examination of his place at home, as master and husband; and outwardly, towards a political stance of opposition against the *Swadeshi* ban on foreign goods, coercion of local farmers and tradesmen who refuse to cooperate, and the xenophobic hysteria that the movement incites. Justified in his truth-convictions, Nikhil emerges as the guardian of inherited values and social formations, and also, paradoxically, as the modern opponent of the nativist myth-making, superstition, and iconicity that Sandip plays upon to create the invented tradition of his movement. Nikhil's voice resonates with that of the poet-speaker in no. LXXXIV of *Gitanjali* we heard before:

> There are many in this world whose minds dwell in brick-built houses, – they can afford to ignore the thing called the outside. But my mind lives under the trees in the open, directly receives upon itself the messages borne by the free winds, and responds from the bottom of its heart to all the musical cadences of light and darkness. (*HW* 312)

If the 'outside' – or the 'world' – is defined by Sandip and in his terms, Nikhil would have no part in it. His response, however, is not withdrawal, but a struggle, through inwardness, to free the 'world' from its political bondage and release it back into nature. In this release, the contemplative man, living the life of the 'mind' rather than that of the body, finds his secure place; 'home', as the inner self, and the 'world' in nature are continuous, the passages between the two uninterrupted and mellifluent. In similar manner, Desai's acute observations about the degradation of the environment and social relations are disrupted by moments when nature returns in splendour through images of elemental differences and correspondence, light and darkness, climactic and seasonal changes, and diurnal movements that remember the romantic pastorality of Bengali poetry and Tagore's songs which are written so much under their influence.

In the triangulated romance narrative, which is the most observable discourse of the novel, Bimala figures as the conventional site of masculinist contest. This discourse is disrupted not only by Nikhil's eventual resignation of his traditional role as her master and guide, but also by the ambivalence in Sandip between seducer and worshipper of her as the embodiment of 'mother-nation'. She is created by both Nikhil and Sandip, and yet she moves beyond this subjected place within the home and allocated place in patriarchal discourse outwards to assume an inspirational role as maternal symbol of the nationalist movement. Consistent with Tagore's complications of home/world, inside/outside, it is also a passage defined by an intensifying realization of the self as a core of passions struggling to be free of the confines of an inherited place, and an expressiveness that displaces an earlier rhetoric of self-effacement and dependency. 'Who could have thought that so much would happen in this one life?' she asks, and continues,

> I feel as if I have passed through a whole series of births ... I knew there would be words between us when I made up my mind to ask my husband to banish foreign goods from our market. But it was my firm belief that I had no need to meet argument by argument, for there was magic in the very air about me. Had not so tremendous a man as Sandip fallen helplessly at my feet ...? Had I called him? No, it was the summons of that magic spell of mine ... Truly have I realized how a goddess feels when she looks upon the radiant face of her devotee.
> With the confidence begotten of these proofs of my power, I was ready to meet my husband like a lightning-charged cloud ... But I could find nothing in him which I could touch. I felt as unreal as a dream – a dream which would leave only the blackness of night when it was over. (*HW* 136–7)

Bimala has taken large strides from her initial humility – or the adoption of a self-identity imposed by tradition – to this moment of assurance in her own power, not only as woman, but, more significantly, as goddess. On the other hand, the vascillations between confidence and insecurity, vis-à-vis her developing relations with Sandip and Nikhil, continue to locate her on insecure ground. In a necessary return to the 'inside' of her allocated home and encounter with her husband, her assurance in her magical power can quickly dissolve in the helplessness of total exclusion, and dissolution of self.

In many ways, Bimala's 'stepping out' from *purdah* into the world as mystical icon of the nationalist cause is the defining movement of the novel to which the passages of both Nikhil and Sandip are coordinated. From zamindar's wife to 'mother-nation': as allegorical figure, Bimala symbolizes the hesitant entries of traditional India into modernity via the jagged course of nationalism. However, the novel also suggests, according to Tagore's biographers, 'his tangled emotions about the 1905 Swadeshi Movement'.[14] The representation of Sandip in his monstrous energy, Nikhil's resolute dissociation, and the fact that the novel ends tragically – in the social upheaval of communalist riots embroiling both Muslims and Hindus, the disgrace and disappearance of Sandip, Bimala's humiliation, and the fatal injury of Nikhil: all these point to Tagore's profound unease and criticism of the nationalistic movement as it was unfolding in Bengal. In her Introduction to a 1985 reprint of *The Home and the World*, Desai refers to the novel as 'a participant in the political storm that had gathered over India ... and of which Tagore was at the vortex' (*HW* 8). The comments by Desai and Tagore's biographers point to the larger issue of the intellectual and writer in a public crisis, and the engagement of a literary work in the course taken by the radical politics of its own time. *The Home and the World* can be seen as a refusal of solidarity with the nationalistic cause, an act of conscience that puts the weight of Tagore's international reputation against a movement lauded by many of his fellow writers in the West, and in so doing, also puts that reputation in jeopardy.

As Desai recalls in the Introduction, the novel attracted the hostility of a Marxist critic like Georg Lukács who called it 'a petit bourgeois yarn of the shoddiest kind' demonstrating that Tagore 'lacks the imagination even to calumniate convincingly and effectively, as Doestoevsky, say, partly succeeded in doing in his counter-revolutionary novel, *Possessed*', and the more liberal, though no less disparaging observation by E. M. Forster that 'the World proved to be a sphere ... for a boarding-house flirtation that masks itself in patriotic talk'. Both critics also deplore the language of the novel: it moves 'amid the sluggish flow of [Tagore's] own tediousness', according to Lukács, and to Forster, it is full of 'Babu sentences'.[13] The political objections to the novel, which are clearly oriented by certain assumptions about class and class-struggle, resonate with similar criticisms of Desai's own work. Her Introduction performs the dual task of explicating the coercive and ruinous power of the nationalistic movement which the novel contests, and which enables it, in Desai's view, to remain 'so astonishingly relevant' to this day, and the 'highly rhetorical' nature of the Bengali language which came across in translation as ornate, archaic, and artificial (*HW* 8–12).

There is no question that in this introduction, as in others to Tagore's works, Desai's enthusiasm and admiration for her predecessor are genuine and deeply felt. What is equally at stake is that in her invocations of Tagore – as realist, as a writer who crosses from India into the world of letters in English, as the target of attack by left-wing critics in the West – Desai also maps the ground in which and on which her own work has been received and judged. The search for Tagore involves not only the rehabilitation of a writer whose international fame has seemed ephemeral, and whose achievement as writer and public intellectual has remained largely unrecognized as his work becomes consigned to a passing phase of western literary fashion. To ask and address the question, what is the political work performed by Tagore's writing in his own and our time? is to mobilize the problematic of how Desai – a bourgeois writer and creator of middle-class characters – and the subjects she fictionalizes can be located in a postcolonial discourse that puts a premium on marginality, radical resistance, and activist agency as the criteria of judging a literary work's contemporary relevance. *Fasting, Feasting* is dedicated 'To Those Whose Stories I've Told'. Unlike *The Village by the Sea*, which states that it is 'based on fact', the dedication to her latest novel suggests that Desai has become much more wary and circumspect. But there is little compromise about the insistence on a referentiality in truth of her fiction, and if the narrative of the horrors of the dysfunctional middle-class Indian family and the abjection of its subjects would irritate both postcolonial activist and ethnic or nationalist apologists, then it is a risk which Desai seems well prepared to take.

Notes

INTRODUCTION

1. Corinne Demas Bliss, 'Against the Current: A Conversation with Anita Desai', *Massachusetts Review*, 29 (1988), 527.
2. Bliss, 'Against the Current', 522.
3. Kirsten Holst Petersen interview 'Anita Desai', *Kunapipi*, 6:3 (1984), 83.
4. Petersen interview, 84.
5. Bliss, 'Against the Current', 522–3.

CHAPTER 1. AT HOME IN INDIA

1. In an interview, Desai says she 'can't bear the sight of' two of her earlier books, *Cry, the Peacock* (1963) and *Bye-Bye, Blackbird* (1971), 'because they're pure emotion, pure, uncontrolled, rampant emotion...so immature, so callow' (Bliss, 'Against the Current', 525). The same may be said of *Voices in the City* (1964), which is sub-Lawrentian in its supposedly passion-inspired outbursts and the rather convoluted emotional gymnastics that the interior monologues reveal.
2. Feroza Jussawalla and Reed Way Dasenbrock (interviewers and eds), *Interviews with writers of the Post-colonial world* (Jackson and London: University Press of Mississippi, 1992), 159.
3. In another interview, Desai notes that 'Surface Textures' is 'about a man who doesn't set out to be a Guru, has no philosophy at all and yet turns into one because that is what people want of him' (Florence Libert, 'An Interview with Anita Desai', *World Literature Written in English*, 30:1, Spring 1990, 53). Despite this authorial explication, it is the case that Harish's intentionality, or lack of it, is not actually revealed in the text itself.

4. The reference to Eliot is entirely germane to an understanding of the modernist tenor of the short story, and indeed of other Desai novels like *Clear Light of Day* and *Baumgartner's Bombay*, both of which use quotations from Eliot as epigraphs.

5. Tagore's writing is a frequent reference point in Desai's works. See her article 'Re-reading Tagore', *Journal of Commonwealth Literature*, 29:1 (1994), 5–14. For an interesting discussion of her reading and views of Tagore, see Lalita Pandit, 'A Sense of Detail and a Sense of Order: Anita Desai Interviewed by Lalita Pandit', in *Literary India: Comparative Studies in Aesthetics, Colonialism, and Culture*, ed. Patrick Colm Hogan and Lalita Pandit (Albany, NY: State University of New York Press, 1995), esp. 166–7.

6. In her book, *Realism and Reality* (New Delhi: Oxford University Press, 1985), Meenakshi Mukherjee comments on the liberal bourgeois class background of Indo-English writers, and their aim to use fiction as a means of championing social reform. See also the collection of essays in *The New Indian Novel in English: A Study of the 1980s*, ed. with an introduction by Viney Kirpal (New Delhi: Allied Publishers Ltd, 1990).

7. The controversies within India surrounding the use of English have intensified considerably since the publication of *The Village by the Sea* in 1982. The colonial legacy of English, its neo-colonial status as the language of education and social privilege, and its situation vis-à-vis resurgent Hindi as majority language and other indigenous Indian languages are issues discussed and debated in Svati Joshi (ed.), *Rethinking English: Essays in Literature, Language, History*, (New Delhi: Trianka, 1991).

8. Raja Rao, 'Language and Spirit', Author's Foreword to *Kanthapura* (1963), repr. in Bill Ashcroft, Gareth Griffiths, Helen Tiffin (eds), *The Post-colonial Studies Reader* (London: Routledge, 1995), 296–7.

9. Ibid., 297.

10. Bliss, 'Against the Current', 529.

11. Rabindranath Tagore, *Nationalism* (1917; Calcutta: Rupa & Co., 1992), 15.

12. Ibid., 14–15.

CHAPTER 2. WOMEN IN INDIA

1. 'A Secret Connivance', *Times Literary Supplement*, 14–20 September 1990, 972, 976.

2. Ibid., 976.

3. Ibid.

4. In the interview with Libert, Desai observes, 'I think you can only

be a social critic quite unconsciously. You have to be chiefly true to yourself, to your own vision. If you are that, if you are uncompromisingly telling the truth about yourself, about your characters and about society, then you become willy-nilly a social critic' (Libert, 'An Interview with Anita Desai', 51.

5. Ramanathan, 'Sexual Violence/Textual Violence: Desai's *Fire on the Mountain* and Shirazi's *Javady Alley*', *Modern Fiction Studies*, 39:1 (Spring 1993), 17–35.

6. See Pandit, 'A Sense of Detail and a Sense of Order', 154.

7. In writing *Fire on the Mountain*, Desai admits that the model before her was Japanese poetry because 'they seemed to be able to compress and to regain the essence of what they wanted to say...' (Libert, 'An Interview with Anita Desai', 48).

8. Giles Gunn, *Beyond Solidarity: Pragmatism and Difference in a Globalized World* (London and Chicago: University of Chicago Press, 2001), 178. Gunn is writing in the context of the dialectic of oppression and liberation in postcolonial fiction, and specifically of Tayeb Salih's *Season of Migration to the North*.

9. Anita Desai, Introduction to *Midnight's Children* (London: Everyman's Library, 1995), xiv.

10. Shirley Chew, 'Searching Voices', in Susheila Nasta (ed.), *Motherlands: Women's Writing from Africa, the Caribbean and South Asia* (London: Rutgers University Press, 1991), 46.

11. Walter Benjamin, 'A Berlin Chronicle' (1932), in *One Way Street and Other Writings*, trans. Edmund Jephcott and Kingsley Shorter (London: New Left Books, 1979), 321.

12. Homi Bhabha (ed.), 'Introduction: Narrating the Nation', in *Nation and Narration* (London: Routledge, 1990), 4 (italics in original).

13. Urvashi Butalia, 'Blood', *Granta*, 57 (Spring 1997), 14. 'Partition' refers to the separation of India, in 1947, into the two post-colonial nation states of India and Pakistan. Since the early nineteenth century, the British ruled India as a single colony with both Hindu and Muslim populations. After Partition, India was supposed to be a secular state while Pakistan would be Muslim. Partition caused a traumatic upheaval as an estimated 12 to 15 million people moved between India and the eastern and western wings of Pakistan within a few months. Around a million people died as a result; many women were raped, homes were destroyed, and acts of bloodshed and violence were committed by both sides. Partition left a legacy of hatred and suspicion between the two nation states and their peoples which endures to this day. See also Urvashi Butalia, *The Other Side of Silence: Voices from the Partition of India* (Durham, NC: Duke University Press, 2000).

14. Anita Desai, 'Passion in Lahore', *New York Review of Books*, 21

December 2000.

15. Chew, 'Searching Voices', 52. See also Rajeswari Mohan, 'The Forked Tongue of Lyric in Anita Desai's *Clear Light of Day*', *Journal of Commonwealth Literature*, 32:1 (1997), 47–65, in which she argues that there is no real reconciliation at the end of the novel, only a sense of the 'paucity of choices available to middle-class women.' (p. 65). Like Chew, Mohan also sees Mira as a representative figure, embodying 'the obscene violence of the postcolonial conjunction of indigenous and colonial patriarchy' (p. 60), and, in this respect, sharing the subjection of both Nanda and Ila in *Fire on the Mountain*.

CHAPTER 3. COMIC MAN, TRAGIC MAN

1. Bliss, 'Against the Current', 537.
2. Petersen interview, 83.
3. There is a significant difference between the novel's representation of Imtiaz, largely mediated by Deven's point of view, and that of the film version, also scripted by Desai in collaboration with Shabrukh Husain (*In Custody*, directed by Ismail Merchant (Merchant Ivory Productions, 1993). In the film, Imtiaz is certainly not plain; her scenes with Nur and the sequence which shows her own performance as poet-singer have a poignancy which is absent from the novel. In the film, her distress about Nur's decline, their marriage, and her frustrated poetic aspirations are highlighted, and enlist Deven's sympathy. Generally speaking, the film is beautifully shot, and has a polished sheen which is very pleasing to the eye. The emphasis of the film-text is much more on beauty as a sensual – and Indian – reality, and this tends to detract from the novel-text's reference of beauty to aesthetic truth.
4. An earlier version of my discussion of *Baumgartner's Bombay* has appeared as an article, 'The Languages of Identity in Anita Desai's *Baumgartner's Bombay*', *World Literature Written in English*, 32:1 (1992), 96–106.
5. 'A Secret Connivance', 972. Although, in the article, Desai was speaking specifically about young girls in India and their early incorporation into traditional cultural orthodoxies so that they identify themselves with certain gender stereotypes, the article's observations are equally germane to an understanding of Baumgartner's identity formation. The article was published in 1990, two years after *Baumgartner's Bombay*.
6. I am grateful to Christopher Hutton for help with the translation.
7. Judie Newman, 'History and Letters: Anita Desai's *Baumgartner's Bombay*', *World Literature Written in English*, 30:1 (1990), 38.

8. Shoshana Felman, 'Education and Crisis, or the Vicissitudes of Teaching', in Shoshana Felman and Dori Laub (eds), *Testimony: Crisis of Witnessing in Literature, Psychoanalysis, and History* (New York: Routledge, 1991), 28, quoted in Gunn, *Beyond* Solidarity, 179. Shoshana Felman is writing in the context of the literature that responds to the Holocaust, or *Shoah*.

CHAPTER 4. *FIRANGHI*

1. Zygmunt Bauman, *Modernity and Ambivalence* (Cambridge: Polity Press, 1991), 55.
2. Anthropology, as an academic discipline, has undergone significant paradigm shifts since the advent of critical anthropology pioneered by Clifford Gertz and James Clifford in the 1970s. Desai's story, published in 1978, would have been written before critical anthropology had thoroughly destabilized the discipline especially in its conceptions of native cultures and its recognition of the power relations between the anthropologist and the native culture in which he or she does fieldwork. See Clifford Geertz (ed.), *Old Societies and New States: The Quest for Modernity in Asia and Africa* (New York: Free Press, 1963), and James Clifford, *The Predicament of Culture* (Cambridge, MA: Harvard University Press, 1988) and *Routes: Travel and Translation in the Late Twentieth Century* (Cambridge, MA: Harvard University Press, 1997).
3. Jussawalla and Dasenbrock, *Interviews with Writers of the Post-Colonial World*, 177.
4. J. M. Coetzee, 'Messages and Silence', *New York Review of Books*, 47:9, 25 May 2000, 35.
5. Meenakshi Mukherjee, 'Divine Passions', *India Review of Books*, 1–7 December 1996, 52.
6. Hermann Hesse, 'Remembrance of India' (1916), in *Autobiographical Writings*, ed. with an introduction by Theodore Ziolkowski, trans. Denver Lindley (London: Jonathan Cape, 1973), 63.
7. An earlier, and much shorter, version of the discussion of the novel has appeared in Elaine Yee Lin Ho, Geetanjali Singh Chanda and Kavita Mathai, 'Women in "India": Four Recent Novels', *Wasafiri*, 26 (Autumn 1997), 58–63.
8. Hermann Hesse, *Siddhartha* (1922), tran. Hilda Rosner (London: Picador, 1998), 98–9.
9. Hesse, 'Remembrance of India', 68.
10. Bliss, 'Against the Current', 522–3. See Introduction to this book, 1.

CHAPTER 5. HOME, WORLD

1. Desai, Introduction to Rabindranath Tagore, *The Post Office*, trans. Krishna Dutta and Andrew Robinson (New York: St Martin's Press, 1996), vi.
2. Desai, 'Re-reading Tagore', 5–14.
3. Ibid., 6.
4. Ibid., 9.
5. Tagore, *Collected Poems and Plays of Rabindranath Tagore* (1936; London: Macmillan, 1988), 12.
6. Ibid., 39.
7. Giyatri Chakravarty Spivak, 'Can the Subaltern Speak?', in C. Nelson and L. Grossberg (eds), *Marxism and the Interpretation of Culture* (Basingstoke: Macmillan, 1988), 271–313.
8. Desai, 'Re-reading Tagore', 11.
9. Coetzee, 'Messages and Silence', 35.
10. Rosemary Marangoly George, *The Politics of Home: Postcolonial Relocations and Twentieth-Century Fiction* (Berkeley and Los Angeles: University of California Press, 1996), 136. The discussion is in ch. 5.
11. Ibid., 132.
12. Ibid., 134.
13. Tagore, *The Home and the World*, trans. Surendranath Tagore, Introduction by Anita Desai (London: Penguin, 1985), 7. Interestingly, Hesse praises Tagore's novel for its 'purity and grandeur', and Bertolt Brecht notes that it is 'a wonderful book, strong and gentle'. See *Rabindranath Tagore: An Anthology*, ed. Krishna Dutta and Andrew Robinson (New York: St Martin's Griffin, 1997), 333.
14. Krishna Dutta and Andrew Robinson, *Rabindranath Tagore: The Myriad-Minded Man* (New York: St Martin's Press, 1996), 193.

Select Bibliography

WORKS BY ANITA DESAI

Cry, the Peacock (London: Peter Owen, 1963; reissued Delhi: Orient Paperbacks, 1980)

Voices in the City (London: Peter Owen, 1964; reissued Delhi: Orient Paperbacks, 1965, 1988).

Bye-Bye, Blackbird (London: Peter Owen, 1971).

Where Shall We Go This Summer? (Delhi: Vision, 1975).

Fire on the Mountain (London: William Heinemann Ltd., 1977, reissued London: Vintage, 1999).

Games at Twilight and Other Stories (London: William Heinemann Ltd, 1978; reissued London: Vintage, 1998).

The Peacock Garden (London: William Heinemann Ltd, 1979; reissued London: Mammoth, 1991, 1997).

Clear Light of Day (London: William Heinemann Ltd, 1980; reissued London: Vintage, 2001).

The Village by the Sea (London: Puffin, 1982; reissued London: Penguin, 1988).

In Custody (London: William Heinemann Ltd, 1984; reissued London: Vintage, 1999).

Introduction to Rabindranath Tagore, *The Home and the World*, trans. Surendranath Tagore (London: Penguin, 1985), 7–14.

Baumgartner's Bombay (London: William Heinemann Ltd, 1988; reissued London: Vintage, 1998).

'Indian Fiction Today', *Daedalus*, 118:4 (Fall 1989), 206–31.

'A Secret Connivance', *Times Literary Supplement* (14–20 September 1990), 972, 976.

'India: The Seed of Destruction', *New York Review of Books* (27 June 1991), 3–4.

In Custody (film) directed by Ismail Merchant, script by Anita Desai and Shabrukh Husain (Merchant Ivory Productions, 1993).

'The Other Voice: A Dialogue between Anita Desai, Caryl Phillips, and Ilan Stavans', *Transition*, 64 (1994), 77–89.

'Re-reading Tagore', *Journal of Commonwealth Literature*, 29:1 (1994), 5–13.

'Publishers, Agents and Agendas', *Library Chronicle*, 25:4 (1995), 96–9.

Introduction to *Midnight's Children* (London: Everyman's Library, 1995), vii–xxi.

Journey to Ithaca (London: William Heinemann Ltd, 1995; reissued London: Vintage, 2001).

Introduction to Rabindranath Tagore, *The Post Office*, trans. Krishna Dutta and Andrew Robinson (New York: St. Martin's Press, 1996), vi–viii.

'The Crack in the China', *New York Review of Books* (8 October 1998), 6–7.

Fasting, Feasting (London: Chatto & Windus, 1999).

Diamond Dust and Other Stories (London: Chatto & Windus, 2000).

'Passion in Lahore', *New York Review of Books*, 21 December 2000 at http://www.nybooks.com/nyrev/

INTERVIEWS WITH ANITA DESAI

Bliss, Corinne Demas, 'Against the Current: A Conversation with Anita Desai', *Massachusetts Review*, 29 (1988), 521–37.

Jussawalla, Feroza and Reed Way Dasenbrock, 'Anita Desai', in *Interviews with Writers of the Post-colonial World*, conducted and edited by Feroza Jussawalla and Reed Way Dasenbrock (Jackson and London: University Press of Mississippi, 1992), 156–79.

Libert, Florence, 'An interview with Anita Desai', *World Literature Written in English*, 30:1 (Spring 1990), 47–55.

Pandit, Lalita, 'A Sense of Detail and a Sense of Order: Anita Desai Interviewed by Lalita Pandit', in *Literary India: Comparative Studies in Aesthetics, Colonialism, and Culture*, ed. Patrick Colm Hogan and Lalita Pandit (Albany, New York: State University of New York Press, 1995), 158–63.

Petersen, Kirsten Holst, 'Anita Desai', *Kunapipi*, 6:3 (1984), 83–5.

CRITICAL STUDIES AND REFERENCES

Andersen, Benedict, *Imagined Communities: Reflections on the Origin and Spread of Nationalism* (London and New York: Verso, 1983).

Bauman, Zygmunt, *Modernity and Ambivalence* (Cambridge: Polity, 1991).

Benjamin, Walter, 'A Berlin Chronicle' (1932), in *One-Way Street and Other Writings*, trans. Edmund Jephcott and Kingsley Shorter (London: New Left Books, 1979), 293–346.

Bhabha, Homi (ed.), *Nation and Narration* (London: Routledge, 1990).

Butalia, Urvashi, 'Blood', *Granta*, 57 (Spring 1997), 13–22.

Capshaw Smith, Katherine, 'Narrating History: The Reality of the Internment Camps in Anita Desai's *Baumgartner's Bombay'*, *ARIEL: A Review of International English Literature*, 28:2 (April 1997), 141–57.

Chew, Shirley, 'Searching Voices', in Susheila Nasta (ed.), *Motherlands: Women's Writing from Africa, the Caribbean and South Asia* (London: Rutgers University Press, 1991), 43–63.

Clifford, James, *The Predicament of Culture* (Cambridge, MA: Harvard University Press, 1988).

—— *Routes: Travel and Translation in the Late Twentieth Century* (Cambridge, MA: Harvard University Press, 1997).

Coetzee, J. M., 'Messages & Silence', *New York Review of Books*, 47:9 (25 May 2000), 33–5.

Dutta, Krishna and Andrew Robinson, *Rabindranath Tagore: The Myriad-Minded Man* (New York: St Martin's Press, 1996).

—— (eds), *Rabindranath Tagore: An Anthology* (New York: St Martin's Griffin, 1997).

Geertz, Clifford (ed.), *Old Societies and New States: The Quest for Modernity in Asia and Africa* (New York: Free Press, 1963).

George, Rosemary Marangoly, *The Politics of Home: Postcolonial Relocations and Twentieth-Century Fiction* (Berkeley and Los Angeles: University of California Press, 1996).

Gunn, Giles, *Beyond Solidarity: Pragmatism and Difference in a Globalized World* (London and Chicago: The University of Chicago Press, 2001).

Hesse, Hermann, 'Remembrance of India' (1916), *Autobiographical Writings*, ed. with an introduction by Theodore Ziolkowski, trans. Denver Lindley (London: Jonathan Cape, 1973).

—— *Siddhartha* (1922), trans. Hilda Rosner (London: Picador, 1998).

Ho, Elaine Yee Lin, 'The Languages of Identity in Anita Desai's *Baumgartner's Bombay'*, *World Literature Written in English*, 32:1 (1992), 96–106.

Ho, Elaine Yee Lin, Geetanjali Singh Chanda and Kavita Mathai, 'Women in "India": Four Recent Novels', *Wasafiri*, 26 (Autumn 1997), 58–63.

Huggan, Graham, 'Philomela's Retold Story: Silence, Music, and the Post-Colonial Text', *Journal of Commonwealth Literature*, 25:1 (1990), 12–23.

Joshi, Svati (ed.), *Rethinking English: Essays in Literature, Language, History* (New Delhi: Trianka, 1991).

Kirpal, Viney, 'An Image of India: A Study of Anita Desai's *In Custody'*, *ARIEL: A Review of International English Literature*, 17:4 (October 1986), 127–38.

—— (ed.), *The New Indian Novel in English: A Study of the 1980s* (New

Delhi: Allied Publishers Ltd, 1990).

Mohan, Rajeswari, 'The Forked Tongue of Lyric in Anita Desai's *Clear Light of Day*', *Journal of Commonwealth Literature*, 32:1 (1997), 47–65.

Mukherjee, Meenakshi, 'Towards Liberation: Four Recent Novels from India', *Westerly*, 4 (December 1983), 66–72.

—— *Realism and Reality* (New Delhi: Oxford University Press, 1985).

—— 'Divine Passions', *India Review of Books*, 1–7 December 1996.

Newman, Judie, 'History and Letters: Anita Desai's *Baumgartner's Bombay*', *World Literature Written in English*, 30:1 (1990), 37–46.

Parker, Michael and Roger Starkey (ed.), *Postcolonial Literature: Achebe, Ngugi, Desai, Walcott* (New York: St Martin's Press, 1995).

Ramanathan, Geeta, 'Sexual Violence/Textual Violence: Desai's *Fire on the Mountain* and Shirazi's *Javady Alley*', *Modern Fiction Studies*, 39:1 (Spring 1993), 17–35.

Rao, Raja, 'Language and Spirit', Author's Foreword to *Kanthapura* (1963), repr. in Bill Ashcroft, Gareth Griffiths and Helen Tiffin (eds), *The Post-colonial Studies Reader* (London: Routledge, 1995), 296–7.

Spivak, Giyatri Chakravarty, 'Can the Subaltern Speak?', in C. Nelson and L. Grossberg (eds), *Marxism and the Interpretation of Culture* (Basingstoke: Macmillan, 1988), 271–313.

Tagore, Rabindranath, *The Home and the World*, trans. Surendranath Tagore, Introduction by Anita Desai (London: Penguin, 1985).

—— *Collected Poems and Plays of Rabindranath Tagore* (1936; London: Macmillan, 1988).

—— *Nationalism* (1917), with an Introduction by E. P. Thompson (London: PaperMac, 1991; Calcutta: Rupa & Co., 1992).

Index

Printed and bound by CPI Group (UK) Ltd, Croydon, CR0 4YY

13/04/2025

14656596-0003